To Vira...
or no one else.
J. H. (xxx Gordon.)

BORN   1913

Labour's Visionary:
LORD HIRSHFIELD

The coat of arms of Lord Hirshfield of Holborn

Labour's Visionary: LORD HIRSHFIELD

Godfrey Gideon

RICHARD COHEN BOOKS · London

British Library Cataloguing in Publication Data:
A catalogue record for this book is available from the British Library

Copyright © 1998 by Lady Hirshfield

ISBN 1 86066 127 0

First published in Great Britain in 1998 by
Richard Cohen Books
7 Manchester Square
London W1M 5RE

1 3 5 7 9 8 6 4 2

Typeset in Sabon by MATS, Southend-on-Sea, Essex

Printed in Great Britain by
T. J. Press International Ltd, Padstow, Cornwall

I greatly respected Desmond's vision for Labour and the Trades Unions, and beyond that, he was a charming person and dear friend.

Elizabeth Longford

Contents

———————————

Contents

List of Illustrations

Between pages 52 and 53

Drawings appear on pp 9, 82-3, 183 and 189

The publishers are grateful to Lady Hirshfield for permission
to reproduce pictures from her personal collection.

Preface

BY LORD CALLAGHAN

This account of Desmond Hirshfield's life was inspired by
Bronia, his wife, and is testimony to her overwhelming,
lifelong love for him and of him for her. Although the book
is focused on Desmond, their two lives were so intertwined
that it becomes an affectionate record of both of them.
Desmond: tall, slim, courteous, deliberate, reserved, a
chartered accountant by profession and a conservative by
nature. Bronia: bubbling, impetuous, imaginative, born in
the Ukraine, brought up in pre-war, anti-semitic Poland – a
rebel against the restrictions placed on their daughters by
Jewish fathers.

Desmond was one of the first, thirty years ago, to
understand the impact that automation and the computer
age would have on the lives of working people, on the
flexibility of labour, and he warned the Trade Unions, who
were his clients, to modernise themselves whilst they had
time. They did not heed his advice.

His principles were strong, but he was never an ardent party politician. His instincts were generous but he always had an eye to account for every penny spent. He was an enthusiastic worker for all Jewish charities but, until just before the end, was not intense in the observance of his religion.

Desmond Hirshfield did great service for the Labour Movement – Party and Trade Unions – overhauling management structures, introducing improved financial methods, devising a Trade Union unit trust for their special needs.

He was happy when his public services were rewarded with a peerage, which he savoured to the end. This book is an excellent reminder of how he was.

James Callaghan

June 1997

Prologue

BY BRONIA HIRSHFIELD

There may be no necessity for another political biography, yet without such a book the story of a man of quiet but nevertheless far-reaching influence in politics and finance would go unnoticed.

Modern British social democracy is a pattern much copied in various guises. Its 'export' has survived competition from Bolshevik ideologues trying to gain 'market penetration' in the developing countries. There is no doubt that Desmond Hirshfield was very much a part of this British export drive and indeed initiated many of the ideas since taken up and in fashion today in these countries.

As early as the 1960s he was propagating the idea of what today is known as the Stakeholder's Society. This concept combines the two pillars of the modern Labour movement: the social consequences of an increasingly automated society; and workers' participation in the vast technological changes that society has inevitably undergone. Desmond

I

was a prophet of such changes in the 1950s and 1960s, lecturing on these subjects to representatives of both capital and labour.

At the same time, his formation of the Trades Union Unit Trust was his practical early expression of such change. He had the ear of, and was indeed encouraged by, Prime Minister Harold Wilson and his Ministers.

However, even a public man has a private life and Desmond's was spent in unshakeable love with me, Bronia, his partner and wife of forty-three years.

My early life – a story of struggle and of emigration from Poland to Palestine and then to England – is also told in this book.

Introduction

For Bronia, life changed when she met Desmond Hirshfield. He was thirty-six, she was thirty-four, and both had broken marriages behind them. They married in July 1951 and her memory of their years together is of mutual devotion and unblemished bliss, until the ravages of age multiplied and his health collapsed: 'We went everywhere together, did everything together, talked over everything together late into the night. When he became ill and was taken to hospital, I went in with him.' And when he died in December 1993, if she had had her way, she would have been buried with him.

They made a handsome couple. He was tall, erect, fair-haired with blue eyes and an air of self-assurance, which, in his younger days, gave him a commanding presence. The air was slightly contrived, for he was easily hurt and, when hurt, was not easily assuaged. She was petite, with light brown hair, green eyes, a neat figure, a determined chin and a presence out of all proportion to her size. There was also a zestful, restless quality about her, so that she seemed animated even in repose.

They spent their honeymoon at the annual conference of the Trade Union Congress in Blackpool. Desmond, who was a senior partner in Hesketh Hardy Hirshfield, a firm of chartered accountants, numbered the Labour Party and several large unions among his clients, and he had to deliver the annual audit not as a mere statement but in the form of a financial review. While the men were in conference or at the bar, Bronia spent much of her time with the wives.

It sounds like a baptism by boredom. However, Bronia learned a lot and claims to have enjoyed it, even to have revelled in it. But then she enjoyed everything as long as Desmond was around, and their years were shaped by the conferences of the Labour Party and the TUC, the National Union of this and the Amalgamated Union of that, while their conversation became bedecked with initials: the NUM, the NUR, USDAW and NATKE, the ETU and the WFFTU.

She was soon familiar with all their seaside venues – Margate and Morecambe, Bournemouth and Yarmouth, Brighton and Clacton, Blackpool and Weston-super-Mare – with sand and spray, chill winds and sea air, pier pavilions and winter gardens. With her bright smile, spirited personality and elegant coiffure, she became one of the ornaments of the conference circuit and a favourite with press photographers on the lookout for a colourful picture.

Her favourite event, however, was the Durham Miners' Gala in July, which was celebrated by the mining communities of north-east England with processions, banners and brass bands thrusting their slow way through the narrow, crowded streets, with the brass gleaming and the bandsmen sweating in the bright sunshine. From what Bronia remembers, the sun always shone on the Gala, and the Durham miners – even though the mines are no more – have a unique place in her affections.

There was almost a religious fervour to the occasion, which reminded her of the Corpus Christi processions in Poland, her childhood home, except that religious processions in Poland filled had her with dread because they were sometimes accompanied by attacks on the local Jews. The Durham Gala however was a source of pleasure.

It followed the same pattern year after year: the leaders of the Labour movement would be grouped together, shoulder to shoulder, on the balcony of the Royal County Hotel overlooking the processional route. Journalists would sometimes measure the standing of the different personalities by their different positions on the balcony, much as Kremlinologists would speculate on the standing of different members of the Politburo by their place on Lenin's mausoleum. But they could not quite work out Desmond's place. He was a joker in the pack, not a miner, not a unionist, not a politician, but an imposing presence, with his well-cut suit and his clean-cut features. He was obviously a man of influence. After the procession there was lunch at the hotel, with the guest list providing a roll-call of the power-holders and power-brokers in the Labour Party.

Desmond stemmed from a Conservative family. However, once he became professionally involved in the work of the trade union movement, he moved to the left, though not too far. He was certainly no doctrinaire Marxist or even a pinkish socialist, and, according to Bronia, he joined the Labour Party out of sympathy for the plight of the working man. He always had a strong sense of social justice, she explains, and became familiar with what was happening to Britain only when he began to work for the unions.

Desmond did not believe in 'the two sides of industry', for he felt that capital and labour had a common interest and should be acting as one. He devoted a good part of his professional life – not always with success – to bringing them together.

In 1951 six years of Labour rule gave way to a new Tory Government, and England began to emerge from the post-war years of austerity and hardship and to live a little. The Hirshfields lived well and entertained lavishly, and their home in Hanover Gate Mansions became a favourite meeting place for Labour politicians, trade union leaders, industrialists, bankers, economists, journalists and lawyers.

Desmond's manner, appearance and lifestyle did not go with the Labour image of the 1950s, and he could have served as the epitome of the 'champagne socialist'. However, this was also true of several left-wing members of the Party, like his friend Nye Bevan, and, while he believed in greater equality, he saw no reason why he should deny himself or his friends the benefits of inequality while they lasted.

Labour did not have many sympathisers in the business world, so Desmond was inevitably drawn into the inner councils of the Party. He helped to reorganise both its administration and finances, and was on close terms with all the Party leaders, from Clement Attlee to James Callaghan.

In 1961, in the face of considerable opposition, he launched the Trades Union Unit Trust, which, as we shall see, became an important source of revenue to the trade union movement. He was also among the first to recognise the threat to employment posed by the growth of auto-mation and in 1962 he set up the Foundation on Auto-mation and Employment. In 1967 he was raised to the peerage.

Asked later if the honour had come as a surprise, Desmond said – only half-jokingly – that he was surprised it hadn't come sooner. It was certainly no surprise to Bronia.

She was a profound believer in fate or, as she would put it in Yiddish, it was *'bashert'*.

From the day she met Desmond, she saw him as a prince in the making and the honour merely confirmed her belief. However, she felt that even fate needed a helping hand and though she was naturally hospitable and loved company, her lavish entertainments were essentially devised to advance his career. All her energies were focused on his needs, and though he was fairly ambitious himself, he was almost retiring compared to the hopes she had for him. She was, as she is at times prepared to admit, possibly a little over-zealous in this respect. At others, she insists that she did no more and no less than might be expected of a loyal wife. What was perhaps more to the point, she felt that she was answering an inner summons.

She was in tears when he took his seat in the House of Lords attired in scarlet and ermine. At the State Opening of Parliament later that year, she wore a long satin gown and a diamond tiara. She had come a long way from Tomaszow in Poland.

Desmond had a few intimate friends and confidants, but Bronia had none. Her whole being was part of his, her whole life entwined with his. She described herself as wife and mistress, but she was also a votary, and she approached him not only with love but adoration. She would stand on the balcony of their flat as he left for work in the morning and would be there to wait for his return.

All the watches of her day and night were determined by his needs, and yet she regarded him as her creation, a good man, a kind man, an able man and a determined man. After his death in 1993 her life's work was gone, and she has since devoted what energies she has to keeping his memory alive, not only for his sake but for hers. She can hardly complete a sentence without making some reference to him. She visits

7

his grave regularly and tends it meticulously, but still refuses to accept the fact that he is no more. Nor will she have anyone to stay with her in case they should disturb his ghost or her reveries. And she regards any attempt to offer consolation or comfort, any suggestion that she still has a life to live, as an impertinence or, worse, a wilful intrusion upon her grief, though Desmond himself had told her a few years earlier: 'You're still lively, still attractive, and you'll have a bit of money. You're a catch. If anything happens to me, I think you should marry again.'

The books and papers in his study are still in place. The books he read in bed are still on his bed-side table. His suits and coats are still on their hangers. His hats are in one cupboard, his shirts in another, his hand-made shoes in a third, including a tiny pair he wore as a child. The pictures he painted on holiday, or in his occasional free hours, line the walls, and the heavy walking sticks he used towards the end of his life are to be found everywhere. His drinks are still in the cocktail cabinet. His Rolls-Royce is still in the garage. Their flat has become a shrine.

Bronia sometimes looks back on their years together and their ascent from obscurity to eminence – she from a small provincial town in Poland, he from an impoverished family in Birmingham – and wonders if it wasn't all a dream.

One of Desmond's sketches of Les-Bains-de-Gaz

I

The Hirshfield Clan

———————

The founding father of the Hirshfield clan – and it is a fairly large one – was Tobias Hirschfeld, as he was known and as some of his progeny are known still. He was born in Podgurz, a small town in the eastern reaches of the Austro-Hungarian empire, in about 1850 and came to Britain when he was fifteen.

Many Jewish immigrants from eastern Europe had a pogrom among their folk memories. There were none in Podgurz, for the Hapsburgs were not the Romanovs, but there was poverty and hardship and Tobias moved to the West to better himself. This he did in a fairly brisk manner. He arrived in Liverpool, hungry and penniless, and made for the nearest synagogue, where he was offered food and accommodation. A few days later he found work with a local jeweller.

He was a bright, energetic and determined youngster, for he quickly learned the trade and moved on to Nottingham, where at the age of eighteen or nineteen he married Rosa, the daughter of a local jeweller, who seemed to have been a man of substance and presumably gave his son-in-law a helping hand. A few years later Tobias settled in Birmingham, where he set up on his own as a jeweller and diamond dealer. He eventually branched out into Hatton Garden, London, as a manufacturing jeweller – where his company is still in business – and attained a standard of living he could not have dreamt of in Podgurz.

Tobias was a devout Jew. The first commandment in Scripture is 'Be fruitful and multiply', and multiply he did. He and Rosa had eleven children – five boys and six girls – of whom eight (four sons and four daughters) survived beyond infancy.

Their oldest son Meyer emigrated to South Africa, where he attained some prosperity, but died at about the age of forty. Their second son Adolph became a dentist, while the third, Alex, went into the family business, which he was later to take over from his father. Leopold, the youngest, born in 1888, became a salesman dealing in greeting-cards, collar studs, hosiery – anything which found a market and quite a few things which did not – and spent much of his time on the road. He could not have been particularly successful, for he joined his brother Adolph as a dental mechanic for a time and eventually became a dentist himself.

Like Adolph, Leo never actually qualified as a dentist, but in the early years of the century there was no statutory need for such qualifications. He opened surgeries in Cardiff, Merthyr Tydfil and Aberdare, and built up a considerable clientele among miners. He could, if need be, drill a tooth and make a filling, but he was rarely called upon to do anything more elaborate than extractions, which he performed by the most rudimentary means.

It was hard work, and though fastidious in dress, he would sometimes come away from his surgery covered in coal-dust. However, he prospered after a fashion.

He later moved back to Birmingham and finally to London, but by then qualified dentists began to edge out the unqualified ones, especially in the capital. He became a Licentiate of the Institute of Hygiene, but his certificate, though impressive, did not amount to a dental diploma. Thus his practice gradually declined and he moved out of dentistry to become manager of a fur company, which processed the pelt of the muskrat to produce musquash and which was said to be a pioneer in its field. It may have been too far ahead of its time for, after a burst of prosperity, it went bankrupt. By then Leo was a family man with three children. Desmond, born in 1913; Norman, in 1915; and Joan, something of an afterthought, in 1920.

Photographs of Leo as a bachelor show a tall, handsome, lordly figure, usually in a top hat, white gloves and a frock-coat, with a carnation in his buttonhole, the complete Edwardian dandy, something of a Burlington Bertie, and, like Burlington Bertie, without the money to go with the style. However, photographs in those days were not casual snaps: they were carefully posed and suggested aspirations rather than reality.

Leo loved the music hall and in the course of his travels he came upon a singer called Lily Black. Tall and vivacious, she had been a child performer in Drury Lane and had appeared with Charlie Chaplin and Dan Leno, or so she claimed. Family lore hath it that Chaplin proposed to her and that with rare prescience she replied: 'No thank you, I'd only be the first of many.' Some fifty years later she saw him dining in the Savoy Grill, an elderly, white-haired figure with an attractive young wife. At the insistence of her family, she went over to greet him. He glanced at her without recognition, exchanged an embarrassed look with his wife and returned to his meal.

Leo was introduced to Lily by his brother Alex while she was in pantomime in Birmingham, when she was still in her teens, and was overwhelmed by both her appearance and her performance. He returned the next night and the next, and then followed her round the country, waiting for her, bouquet in hand, at the stage door. This was no passing infatuation. He fell deeply in love with her, and she with him.

Lily was born in St Martin's Lane on 11 January 1889, the daughter of Edward Blackford, a clothier. She was extremely pretty and fairly gifted as a child and matured quickly into a striking young woman with full sensuous lips, a cascade of golden curls which went over her shoulders, and a beguiling little-girl-lost look in her blue eyes which she carried well into womanhood.

She was only fifteen when she assumed one of the juvenile leads in *Robinson Crusoe* at a Christmas pantomime in Bradford and was an immediate success. One critic wrote: 'First and foremost in my susceptible heart I enshrine Miss Lily Black, the Principal Girl. She is delightful, sprightly, without being vulgar, she has a sweet voice and a personality which would melt the heart of a Free Church Councillor.' Another critic was equally enthusiastic: 'She is a tasty, tuneful, trickful little girl who would warm the heart of the Czar himself.'

Lily possibly peaked early, for having shown sufficient talent to obtain a leading role in the provincial theatre, she was not talented enough to secure any major London engagement. Max Tyler, of the British Musical Hall Society and an authority on the subject, has scoured the theatre directories of the period without finding any reference to her at all. 'Which doesn't mean she wasn't on stage,' he says, 'but it does mean that she wasn't particularly prominent. In any case, if she had been well known, I would have heard of her myself.'

But whatever the measure of her talents, there is no question about her attractions. She was an extremely good-looking woman, shapely, warm and lively, and remained so into old age.

Leo's father, however, who by then was a leading member of the Birmingham Jewish community and a stalwart of the Singers' Hill Synagogue, was not particularly taken with Lily, or rather the idea of her, for at this point they had not even met. What was more, he refused to meet her.

By then, Leo must have been a source of anxiety to his father. He was not the observant Jew his father hoped he would be. He could not make a steady livelihood and the normal route to solvency for a good-looking young man without money was to marry a woman with money. Lily had none. What was worse, she was a music-hall singer, and music halls and music-hall artists were regarded by devout Jews – and not only devout ones – with disapproval if not disdain. And to cap it all, she wasn't Jewish. Any one of these factors would have occasioned displeasure, but the last was a calamity. Birmingham was never a hot-bed of Jewish orthodoxy, but the least that congregants of Singers' Hill expected of one another was that their children marry into the faith.

The Rothschilds had begun to marry out of the faith by then, but for a middle-class Jew to contemplate any such step was unheard of. Leo himself, however, was fairly orthodox in his way, or at least had every intention of remaining within the fold, and at his behest Lily, a cheerful pagan, agreed to be converted to Judaism.

It was no small commitment for a young woman with her

background and blithe disposition. She underwent a prolonged course of study, learned to read Hebrew, undertook to conform to Jewish usage, went through the ceremony of ritual immersion and was formally received into the Jewish faith on 23 September 1910.

The certificate of conversion marked with the stamp of 'The Bradford Congregation of British and Foreign Jews', reads:

> This is to certify that LEAH LILY BLACK has appeared before us today with a request that she might be received into the synagogue as a proselyte to its faith. She has expressed her intention of remaining faithful to the religion of her adoption and she has declared that the step taken by her is induced by conviction and that she has in no way been influenced thereto by advice from others. In the course of the examination she underwent, she answered most satisfactorily the questions which we have put to her, touching the principles and observance of Judaism which she has practised for a number of years. She is herewith received into the community of Israel as a proselyte of righteousness.

It is signed by Dr Joseph Strauss, rabbi of the synagogue; another man whose name is illegible; and Jacob Moser, a wealthy Jewish philanthropist who was President of the synagogue and Mayor Elect of Bradford.

Leo and Lily were married in the synagogue two days later. It was a bleak little ceremony with barely more than ten people grouped round the bridal canopy. Leo's parents were not among them, and neither were his brothers and sisters. They were Orthodox while the synagogue was Reform. Tobias did not recognise the conversion and virtually disowned his son. They were only reconciled some sixteen years later when Tobias and his wife came down to London to attend Desmond's Barmitzvah at the Brixton Synagogue.

The young people, according to the local papers, went on honeymoon to Palestine, a surprising destination given their limited means. It is possible that Moser, a prominent Zionist and a Santa Claus of a man, may have paid for it, but it was probably one of Leo's flights of fancy. He liked to give the impression that he was doing well and a visit to Palestine sounded better than a week in Harrogate. At the very least, however, it was a pious thought.

Desmond was born in Edgbaston, Birmingham, on 17 May 1913. His father was delighted to have a son and heir, and the measure of his delight may be gauged from a whimsical little letter sent from the George Hotel, Aylesbury:

My darling little Son,
This is my very first letter to you and I hope that your dear mother will keep it, so that when you grow older you may see it and read it out to me.

I hope you have been a good little boy, as you are nearly three weeks old and will soon be going out with your dady [*sic*].

Has mumsie taken you into the garden today?

Well little fellow I must go now and will pray tonight that God will send his guardian angels to watch over and guide you all your life.

From your ever loving dady [*sic*].
Leo

They were a happy family and, whatever the nature of her conversion, Lily kept her undertakings to conform to the Jewish faith both in letter and spirit. As the years passed she even acquired the mannerisms and expressions of the traditional Jewish mother, as one can see from a letter she sent to Leo during the First World War a few years after they married:

My Darling Leo,
I cannot believe tomorrow evening is Yomtoff.
   I wish you a very happy and prosperous New Year and may it please God that this dreadful war will be at an end in the near future and we shall all be at peace.
   It is the first Rosh Hashono we have all been separated. However, please God you will be down on Friday.
   Try to bring me some frying oil from Hills or Greens.
   Trust everything is going well . . .
   Fondest love and kisses,
   From your devoted wife,
        Lily

Yomtoff (or more precisely Yom Tov) is the Yiddish for festival. Rosh Hashono is the Jewish New Year and one of the most sacred occasions in the Jewish calendar. The fact that Leo's travels kept him away from his family suggests how hard he had to work for a living. The letter itself, however, with its repeated references to God, could hardly have been more Jewish in tone or sentiment, while the reference to frying oil suggests that Lily had also mastered Jewish cuisine, for while gefilte fish may be the most Jewish of all Jewish dishes, it is less popular among English Jews than fish dipped in eggs and matzo-meal and fried in oil. In many respects she became a better Jew than Leo and would occasionally complain about his religious shortcomings.

   She stood over the children to make sure that they ate properly and conformed to the basic observances of Jewish life. When the family moved to south London, she became a prominent, active and popular member of the Brixton Synagogue. Lord Mishcon, whose father was rabbi of the synagogue, remembers seeing her regularly with her young daughter in the front row of the ladies' gallery on Saturday mornings: 'An adornment, both of them.'

As her sons grew older, Lily would caution them about going out with non-Jewish girls and would make a scene if they did.

Her marriage, in some respects, was something of a sacrifice to her. She was only twenty-one at the time. She had outgrown the charm attached to child performers, but was still young enough, beguiling enough and talented enough to entertain hopes of establishing a name as an adult performer. However, she gave it all up to marry a man with a shaky past and an uncertain future. Yet if she had any regrets on the matter, she rarely voiced them, at least within the hearing of her children.

They might have enjoyed a stable life and a modest prosperity had Leo been content with what he had, but he was always on the lookout for something better. As a result, they were nearly always on the move, from Birmingham to Cardiff, from Cardiff to Aberdare, from Aberdare to Merthyr Tydfil. Things sometimes did get better, but they did not stay better, and so they moved again from Merthyr Tydfil back to Cardiff, from Cardiff back to Birmingham and thence to Barnes, Herne Hill, Dulwich, West Hampstead and finally to Golders Green. Desmond's younger brother Norman recalls twelve different changes of address in the course of fifteen years.

As a music-hall artist, Lily was used to a peripatetic existence, but she had not been encumbered with children. However, she had not only great love for her husband but a great faith in his ability and judgement. Her faith was not totally misplaced for though they kept having ups and downs, they were generally moving in an upward direction. One of the reasons that they moved so frequently in the early years was that Leo tried to make a small profit from the sale of each home. Unfortunately, his income rarely kept pace with his expenditure. He was among the first men in

England to own a Buick – and a chauffeur – and later he preferred to rent a grand home than to buy a more modest one. Leo and Lily loved display, good food, elegant clothes, expensive hotels and spacious surroundings. Sibling rivalry may also have played its part. His brothers and sisters were doing well and he liked to give the impression that he was doing better.

Desmond inherited something of his father's attitude, for though he was infinitely better off, he lived in rented accommodation for most of his life, though as an accountant he may not have cared to tie up his capital.

Old Tobias Hirschfeld had his main business in London, but preferred to remain in Birmingham in a large house in Selwyn Road surrounded by servants: a rather aloof, distant, unsmiling figure who was regarded by his children and grandchildren with reverence rather than affection. He died in 1934 and left £17,286, a large sum in those days, but given the size of his family not enough for generous handouts. He left £25 to the Singers' Hill Synagogue and nearly everything else upon trust to his widow. He also arranged that each of their grandchildren should receive £1,000 on her death, with the residue to be divided between his surviving children. He had provided for his daughters during his lifetime. He waived a debt of £2,500 owed to him by his son Alexander and left £300 to Adolph. In effect, Leo got nothing.

2

An Active Youth

Desmond's earliest memories as a boy in Wales were of hanging around his father's surgery with its odd smells and crude instruments and extracting gold from extracted teeth. As he said later, 'I began my life in the gold trade.'

The many changes of address meant a disrupted education, six months in this place, a year or two in that, often going over the same ground. He went to seven schools before settling down to a period of sustained education at the City of London, a stately pile overlooking the Thames by Blackfriars Bridge, one of the best schools in the capital and, by Leo's standards, a fairly expensive one.

Desmond was a bookish youngster, but plagued by ill-health. Added to the normal score of childhood maladies was an attack of typhoid fever which nearly killed him and left him vulnerable to further ailments. A little later he went down with double pneumonia, which was again nearly fatal, and as if that wasn't enough he suffered from a mastoid and had to have surgery on his ear.

Bronia, in recounting his litany of disorders – and there were more to follow – is half convinced that the fact that he survived them all was in itself proof that he was destined for greatness. He quickly recovered from most of his illnesses and during the course of his life was normally well, strong and active.

His art teacher at a private school in Cardiff, which he attended when he was eight, thought that he had a promising future, as she wrote to his mother: 'I should think Desmond will develop into a great Artist and Sculptor. If he goes on using his hands and his eyes as well as he does now, I feel sure that with the artistic gifts you have passed on to him he will do well.' He continued to show promise, but, possibly because of her own experience as an artiste, Lily never encouraged him to contemplate a career in the arts, and he was perfectly content to become an accountant.

During his early years, he spent more hours at home than in school and his mother became his constant companion. She nursed him during his illnesses, read to him during his convalescences, played with him and told him stories with such animation that they almost amounted to pantomime performances. The fact that she lavished so much attention on him meant that she may have neglected his younger brother; this possibly led to the strains which later developed between them.

Leo was often away from home, sometimes for weeks on end, and Lily kept a small black book of misdemeanours perpetrated by the children in his absence. Desmond, a sensitive child, was terrified of the book and of his father, who featured in his imagination as a god of wrath, though Norman remembers him as fairly easy-going and thought that Lily was by far the stricter disciplinarian of the two, especially where it came to matters of Jewish observance.

One could argue with Leo, but one hesitated to argue with Lily.

The severity which Desmond noted in his father was possibly due to frustration. His frequent journeys were often attempts to clinch a business deal, but many of his deals remained stubbornly unclinched, and while he tried to present a smiling face to the world he was not always in the best of moods at home. Circumstances improved by the time Desmond was ten. Leo acquired a steady job and a sizeable income as the sales director of Dereta, a large, well-known garment company. They rented a spacious house in Dulwich with several servants and, as we have noted, Desmond entered the City of London School.

Given his poor health and his frequent absences from school, the entry exam required some effort and he needed a private tutor. He worked hard and at the end of 1924 the tutor was able to report:

> I hope Desmond will be successful in his examination. Considering the disadvantages he was up against, he put up a very plucky performance. I wish to assure you and Mrs Hirshfield that I found it very pleasant to work with Desmond. Although I feel I drove him pretty hard, he responded most manfully, and if he keeps on working in that spirit, he is bound to get on at his new school.

He did get on and loved the school, and looked back on his years there with nostalgia, though he did have some embarrassing moments. For example, his mother once knitted him a cardigan of many colours and was so proud of her work that she insisted he wear it to school. As soon as he set foot in the playground, he was subjected to such a barrage of ribaldry and abuse that he took refuge in a dustbin.

When he was fifteen, he was given a large diary as a Christmas present and he made regular entries for some ten weeks. He was in his fourth term in Mortimer House by then and notes with pride that he was elected captain of chess. He does well at games and takes extra lessons in Spanish, music and art. He has frequent walks on his own in Dulwich Park or on Camberwell Green. He speaks of his 'darling mother', but there are no such affectionate references to his father. He listens a lot to the radio, usually to serious programmes (there were hardly any other in 1929). He follows the Test scores in Australia with great attention and comments on England's lack-lustre performance. He goes out to the cinema and theatre, but always in the company of his parents, his brother – two years younger than him – and his sister Joan, who was seven years younger, exceedingly pretty and everyone's darling.

He seems never to venture out of his neighbourhood on his own. There isn't a single reference to friends or companions. They were a close family and he was clearly devoted to his brother and sister, but most boys of fifteen prefer the company of contemporaries. His diary suggests a fairly lonely boyhood, though again recurring spasms of ill-health may have been the source of his isolation. To be one of the crowd, a boy among boys, calls for a certain physical robustness.

There is a reference in his diary to Rosh Chodesh, meaning the new month, which is observed among very Orthodox Jews as a minor festival with special prayers, but is barely noticed by anyone else.

Lord Mishcon, whose father was rabbi of the local synagogue, as has been said, and who was Desmond's contemporary at the City of London, recalls him as religious and pensive, but perhaps a little sanctimonious and priggish. He would be in synagogue with his father and brother on Friday evenings, and on Saturday mornings the whole family would turn up for prayer. He would follow the service closely while most youngsters of his age played around.

The Hirshfields were popular members of the community. They joined enthusiastically in the social and cultural events organised by the synagogue and were greatly missed when they moved to Golders Green.

Desmond was to lose much of his religiosity in later life, only to recover something of it again in old age.

His schooling, as we have seen, was hampered by his frail health. He was very good at English and modern languages – German, French and Spanish – and showed pronounced promise in art, but like many boys who were later to become accountants, he was less than brilliant at maths. At the end of his third term in 1928, he was sixteenth in a class of twenty-eight, and the comment of his maths teacher was, 'Getting on slowly. Has not yet learned to think with precision.' He improved slightly in the following year and when he left school his form master, L. Gilbey, gave him a glowing report and also showed considerable insight into his character:

Mr D. B. Hirshfield was in my class, the Modern Upper Fourth (one of the higher classes in the school) during his last term at the school – Jan. 6 to April 1929. He did so well in the two main subjects of study that as a result of the term's work and the examination he was first (equal) in French and third in German, in a class of thirty boys, many of them hard workers. He also took Spanish three times a week as an extra subject. He was also third in English Literature.

I believe Mr Hirshfield would take the greatest pains with any duties given him and that he would perform them intelligently, and I have the highest opinion of his character.

Desmond, however, had to go on to a crammer, Marcys in Chancery Lane, to improve his grades in maths, and in 1931 he was apprenticed to the small accountancy firm of Duck, Mansfield & Co.

He also read law at London University and, according to Bronia, studied for one year at Heidelberg, where he perfected his German. There are no records to show how he fared in Heidelberg, but he failed his law exams in London.

He was possibly a late developer, for he had a clear mind and, certainly in later years, could think with precision and display very considerable forensic skills in drafting documents and reports. However, he made no attempt to resume his legal studies and, as he put it, 'after I qualified my father thought it was about time I earned a living'.

His father's feelings were not unreasonable, for Desmond did not qualify until 1939. There were several reasons for the long gestation. One of them was a further collapse in health, another was the number and variety of his outside interests.

Leo had joined the Conservative Party shortly after moving to London and stood as a candidate in the Old Kent Ward in the Camberwell Borough elections. This was a few years after the First World War when anything which sounded vaguely German was unacceptable, so he changed his name from Hirschfeld to Hirshfield. He was an impressive figure and an able speaker and was elected. Later, when he moved to Golders Green, he stood as a Conservative for the Hendon Borough Council and was again elected, though his efforts to become Mayor of Hendon proved abortive.

Desmond, in the meantime, became the Master of Revels among young Conservatives in Golders Green and helped to organise a succession of tennis tournaments, car rallies, dinners, dances, balls, cruises, fancy-dress parties and other entertainments, which became the talk of north-west London, as is evident from a report in the *Golders Green Gazette*:

> Tomorrow Saturday, sandwich men will be parading Golders Green with very unusual boards. Look out for them.
>
> They will be advertising one of the strangest functions Golders Green has seen for years. Due to take place at the 'haunted castle of Brent Bridge'.
>
> According to Desmond Hirshfield, this will be a more glamorous, more glorious event than either of his two local successes, last year's Hollywood Ball and the Cruising Ball of three years ago. He is organising it for the Golders Green Conservative Association.

In 1937 he persuaded his beautiful younger sister, then only seventeen, to become Queen of the Ball in a celebration to mark the Coronation of George VI, and not surprisingly she proved a great attraction. By all reports the Ball was yet another success.

Desmond remained active in the local Conservative Party until the outbreak of war, whereas most young Jews of his generation, even from prosperous homes, tended to lean to the left. After the rise of Hitler a few of them even became Communists, though some were to become Conservative in later years. With Desmond the trend was reversed, but his Conservatism appears to have been primarily due to family loyalty. Like his brother, he had been brought into the Party by his father and, as a loyal son, he was anxious to advance his father's political ambitions. If, like most Jews, he was unhappy about Chamberlain's appeasement policies, it did not affect his attitudes to the Party.

Moreover, the Conservatives were socially attractive. They gave the best parties, had the best venues, attracted the prettiest girls, and offered the most scope for Desmond's gaiety and showmanship. The left was earnest, the right was fun.

Desmond's poor health had also left him with the premonition – a mistaken one as it happened – that he wasn't long for this world and he might therefore have felt entitled to any fun that was going. However, this did not mean that he was a mindless hedonist, for he was always conscious of his responsibilities. There was an earnest side to him which surfaced at the most unlikely moments and which occasionally made him sound pompous, but in the main he carried his seriousness lightly.

He was active in the social and cultural life of the Brixton Synagogue when he lived in south London, and of the Hampstead Synagogue when he moved to Golders Green. There was in fact a large synagogue in Dunstan Road, a few hundred yards from his home in Ridgeway, but he preferred Hampstead because, like the Conservative Party, it was more fashionable and attractive. It also answered to his love of splendour, for, with its lofty façade, stained-glass windows and marbled interior, it looked more like a cathedral than a synagogue and had a decorous, almost church-like atmosphere. Dunstan Road, moreover, was favoured by the newer Jewish families, many of whom still spoke with foreign accents and retained foreign ways, whereas in Hampstead Desmond could celebrate his Jewishness without compromising his Englishness.

He was also a leading member of Maccabi, an international organisation established in 1921 to encourage sporting and cultural activities among Jewish youth. He was tall, lean and, though never robust, was always athletic, a keen tennis-player and a good footballer. His athleticism, one must add, was due less to natural agility or vigour than a grim determination to overcome his disabilities, because apart from the troubles with his health, he had trouble with his feet and had to wear special shoes. But he treated his handicaps as a challenge and succeeded to a marvellous degree.

The rise of Hitler and the spread of Nazi racial theories had aroused Jewish consciousness in many people who had moved far from their faith, and a few months after Hitler came to power, Lord Melchett, the son of a Jewish father (Alfred Mond, founder of ICI) who had been raised as a Christian, formally converted to Judaism. His conversion, at a time when anti-Semitism was rife in much of Europe and when many Jews were making desperate efforts to hide their identities, excited international attention and boosted Jewish morale. As a result, he was elected President of the World Maccabi Union.

The Maccabi held an international Maccabiad every four years, modelled roughly on the Olympics, and the games planned for 1934 therefore assumed considerable symbolic significance in Jewish eyes and attracted Jewish athletes of international standing who had hitherto been totally removed from Jewish life. The games were initially to have been held in Cernutti, Romania, but when it was announced that Melchett would be presiding over them, the Romanian government let it be known that it could not be responsible for his personal safety. The games were therefore moved at short notice to Prague.

Desmond was made captain of the British team. He was by no means the top athlete in Maccabi, but he had pronounced organisational ability. He was also of striking appearance and was thought to be an ideal flag-bearer, for with his great height, blond hair and blue eyes, he had what in those days was known as 'Nordic good looks', though the very fact that Maccabi sought to conform to the Germanic ideas of what constituted good looks was in itself a measure of how far Jewish morale had fallen.

Desmond entered for the 200 metres and the long jump, which meant prolonged training sessions. Moreover, the change of venue at short notice meant a frantic re-organisation of schedules and travel plans, and as team captain he was involved in succession of endless meetings. He could not even relax on the journey to Prague as he had to keep an eye on his team like a mother hen with wayward chicks. When the games were over, he sat down to draft a lengthy, detailed report of everything that had gone right, and of a few things which had gone wrong. The effort, given his medical history, was excessive and a few weeks later he was taken seriously ill.

He was sent from one specialist to another and was eventually found to be suffering from tuberculosis. Doctors recommended treatment at a clinic in Davos, Switzerland, where he remained for over a year. He seemed to have made a good recovery and returned to London to resume his studies, but suffered a relapse a few months later and returned to Davos for further treatment.

His prolonged stay in what was a very expensive sana-torium imposed a considerable strain on family finances and he was helped out by his brother who had left school at fourteen and who, though only in his early twenties, was already a successful estate agent. Desmond did not care to be beholden to anyone, and the fact that he had to be assisted by his younger brother gave him a feeling of help-lessness and occasioned a sense of resentment which added to the strains in their relationship.

Another patient at the sanatorium was a young Polish woman from Danzig called Pimy Goldfab, who was bright, large-eyed, full-bodied and vivacious. None of Desmond's letters from Davos survive, but he spent much of his time making sketches and Pimy features in many of them, walking, running, dancing, reading. He seemed to be excited by her every movement.

It is uncertain whether their relationship speeded his recovery or delayed it, but they corresponded after he left Davos. He visited her family in Poland and she came to stay with his in London, but he was still only a student and not in a position to marry, and his father was not in a position to support him. Moreover, tuberculosis in those days was an almost unmentionable blight. His parents had begun to think of Desmond as a chronic invalid and felt that if he was to marry at all, he would need a healthy wife, preferably with a healthy income. Desmond presumably shared their views, and his friendship with Pimy was allowed to lapse.

Pimy returned to Poland and he never saw her again. After the war, he learned that she and her family had perished in Auschwitz and he sometimes blamed himself for her tragic fate.

It was his first serious relationship and it left him deeply affected. Switzerland remained in his imagination as a place of enchantment. He would return to it every year, usually to Davos, and while he rarely, if ever, gave Bronia cause for jealousy, she sometimes resented the ghost of Pimy. Yet it is possible that she may have owed something to Pimy for her own place in Desmond's affections, for they were both Polish and, from what one can gather, fairly similar in appearance, temperament and build.

Desmond's extensive travels had given him more than an inkling of the ferocity and scale of the Nazi menace not only as it affected Germany but as it affected Europe. As he had a good grasp of German, Duck, Mansfield sent him out to work in their Berlin office so that he was able to see the situation at first hand and the extent to which Jews were being pillaged and persecuted, forced out of the professions and commerce and reduced to ruin. Yet even the Jews themselves were not fully aware of the dangers they faced and comforted themselves with the thought that Hitler was a passing phenomenon and that German decency and good sense would eventually assert itself. They soon discovered their mistake and began to scatter in all directions.

Much of the world was closed to them and there were serious restrictions on entry to Britain; but these were gradually, if reluctantly, eased, especially after Germany absorbed Austria and occupied Czechoslovakia. Between 1933 and 1940 around 70,000 Jewish refugees entered the country. At first they came in a trickle, but as the crisis intensified they arrived in a flood. The Jewish community had to set up an emergency headquarters in Bloomsbury House, near London University, to obtain the necessary entry permits and cope with their needs.

Bloomsbury House was a huge building, which in an earlier incarnation had been a hotel. It was not the only centre working for refugees, but it was by far the largest and acted as co-ordinator. Men and women flocked to it from all directions to offer what help they could and by the outbreak of war almost a thousand people, most of them volunteers, some of them newcomers themselves, worked in its rooms and corridors, or overflowed on to the pavements outside, striving frantically to make themselves useful and sometimes impeding the efforts of others in their eagerness and concern. The overall picture was one of zeal rather than order, but in spite of that the centre somehow coped with the tragic situation.

Desmond, who on qualifying as an accountant had rented a small office a few streets away, was inevitably drawn into its work, and not only because of his personal concern for the plight of the refugees. As an accountant, he knew how to deal with the myriad of regulations affecting the transfer of funds and property. He knew the ropes. He was also familiar with German and Germany. Above all, with his air of authority and soft voice, he was a calm and calming presence among people who – for understandable reasons – were often on the brink of hysteria.

Desmond was active at several levels. Until December 1939 refugees were admitted on the understanding that their maintenance would be guaranteed by the Jewish community, and Desmond importuned friends, relations, clients and even casual contacts to act as guarantors. He also busied himself in finding homes and, perhaps most difficult of all, jobs for the newcomers.

Urban unemployment was very high at the time so that it was almost impossible to obtain labour permits, but there was a shortage of farm hands. After negotiations with the National Union of Agricultural Workers and the Ministry of Labour, Desmond helped to work out a scheme which enabled over a thousand Jewish newcomers, all in their late teens or early twenties, to find jobs on the land. Very few of the newcomers had any agricultural skills, or indeed any experience of manual work at all, and he helped to set up hostels and agricultural training centres. These were scattered in different parts of the country and Desmond would visit them frequently to make sure that they were being efficiently run. He was pleasantly surprised to discover how readily and cheerfully the newcomers were adapting themselves to their new situation, and the valuable contributions they were making to agricultural output. It had never occurred to him that Jews could make good farmers.

Some of the hostels served as rudimentary kibbutzim and after the war many of the young people went out to Palestine to set up real ones. Desmond never described himself as a Zionist and never held office in the Zionist movement, but he possibly did more for the rebuilding of Zion than many a Zionist zealot.

After his death Bronia received a letter of condolence from Teddy Kollek, the Mayor of Jerusalem. As a young man Kollek had been closely involved in the international effort to resettle and rehabilitate Jewish refugees, and he described in some detail the help he received from Desmond:

> My great memory of Desmond is that when we needed guarantees that would allow young German Jews to come to England, he did not hesitate to offer his help. He provided guarantees that these young people would not be a burden on the municipal job market but would go to the country and the farms where labour was needed. Desmond's guarantee was accepted by the Department of Labour and enabled us to bring out 3,500 youngsters who had been incarcerated by the Gestapo. Many of these young people eventually found their way to Israel after the war and remain in your husband's debt, as do we all.

Bloomsbury House featured in several autobiographies of the period, but there isn't a single reference to Desmond in any of them. His office diaries, however, are crowded with meetings, appointments in Bloomsbury House, appointments with refugees and appointments with government officials. If he was not a major player, he was certainly an important one. The issue dominated his working days and, one suspects, half his nights.

Desmond, moreover, was too young and inexperienced to hold any of the public offices which would have pushed him into the limelight. He made himself useful rather than conspicuous, and came and went quietly and unobtrusively. In this instance, as in others, he preferred to act behind the scenes, so Kollek's tribute was richly deserved.

It is difficult to get a clear picture of Desmond at this stage of his career. His brother describes him as a young man on the make. Bronia – who only got to know him some ten years later – thinks of him as a selfless and tireless idealist. However, one can possibly get a more objective picture from some of the people who came into contact with him during the refugee crisis.

One was Else Lowenstein, who came to Britain at the age of thirteen. Her father, a prosperous dealer in leather goods, lost his sight in 1932 and, after the rise of Hitler, lost his business. When he arrived in London with his family in 1939, he had little money, few connections and didn't know what to do next. A friend recommended Desmond as an able young accountant who might be able to help him. Else, who had been reading Oscar Wilde at school, regarded Desmond as a Dorian Gray, 'except that Dorian Gray was evil, while Desmond was one of the kindest, most helpful people I've ever met. He radiated goodness. It might be too much to say that he saved our lives, but he saved our sanity.

'My father became one of his clients, but Desmond was far more than an accountant. My father knew very little about English business practices and nothing about all the new rules and regulations. He had to keep phoning Desmond all the time, not only about business matters, but about permits for this and permits for that, but he was always available and always patient, and with a few calls sorted everything out.

'He had time for everyone, and was patient with everyone. If a problem arose, it was always "call Desmond". I'm surprised he never got sick and tired of us. We had been through a frightening time in Germany, and things weren't all that easy in England and just knowing that he was there at the end of the line made us feel more secure.'

Others, hearing of Lowenstein's experience, also came to Desmond, and refugees whom he guided through these early travails eventually prospered and became his most devoted clients.

Desmond's role in Bloomsbury House became fairly crucial once war broke out. Given his medical history, he was unfit for military service and remained in London while many of the other British nationals involved in refugee work vanished into the armed forces. He reorganised the entire running of Bloomsbury House and took its accounts under his control. (He was paid 30 shillings a week towards the cost of his clerk's salary, which may now seem a mean exaction, but at the time he wasn't earning much more than a clerk himself.)

In May 1940, after Hitler invaded Belgium and Holland, some 30,000 refugees were rounded up as 'enemy aliens' and security risks. Some were deported to Australia and Canada, but most were interned at various camps in the British Isles, including the Isle of Man. Desmond – who was not alone in this respect – regarded the whole operation as a fit of madness and did what he could to ameliorate its effects.

Aliens could appeal to Home Office tribunals against internment and Desmond became a liaison officer of the County of Bedfordshire's tribunal. He later claimed in the course of a newspaper interview that he also worked for the Home Office in a secret capacity, which is not at all improbable for, as we have observed, he knew Germany and spoke German. He also looked German, and it is likely that he was involved in singling out aliens who might have harboured Nazi sympathies from the innocent refugees who formed the mass of the internees. The restrictions were gradually eased and the regulations modified, and by 1942 most of the internment camps were closed.

The refugee crisis dominated Desmond's first year in his profession and left him with little time or energy to pursue his private interests. Nevertheless, despite all the cares which fell upon him, he also found time to get married at Hampstead Synagogue, where he had been a member for nearly ten years, in July 1940. Desmond and his new wife, Alma, took a week off for a honeymoon in Bournemouth. However, as he was still coping with the crisis arising out of the internment of Jewish aliens, he remained in daily touch with his office, and on one occasion even made a quick dash back to London.

In the meantime, his father-in-law had helped him to acquire a partnership in the accountancy practice of Hesketh Hardy, which now became Hesketh Hardy Hirshfield (HHH). Hesketh was no more; Hardy, the senior partner – who was born Cohen – remained in Manchester, while Desmond set up office in two gloomy little rooms in the basement of 20 Bedford Row, Bloomsbury. He complained to Hardy about these cramped conditions and pointed out that it was embarrassing to interview clients and difficult to recruit staff in such dingy surroundings, but accountancy offices in those days were rarely palatial and his complaints went unheeded.

The Blitz began a few weeks after he moved in and continued on an almost daily – and eventually nightly – basis until the following June.

He rented a large house in West Heath Close, Hampstead, which suffered a direct hit shortly after he and his wife moved in, but fortunately the bomb failed to explode. Then his office was damaged on 7 September. Two weeks later his parents' home in Golders Green suffered serious damage and he had to find them temporary accommodation in Stratford-upon-Avon.

Desmond went to bed not knowing whether he would wake up in the morning, and went to work not knowing if his office would be intact when he got there. On 15 October a land mine fell on Bedford Row and his office was extensively damaged. For a month or more he had to work from home.

It was a bleak time all round. Staff couldn't always get to work because of the devastation. It wasn't easy to reach clients and clients couldn't always reach him. Phones were often out of order, and lighting and heating sometimes failed. He still had a car, but couldn't always get petrol and the roads were often impassable.

On 18 April 1941 Bedford Row was gutted in a heavy incendiary raid and anything not damaged by fire was ruined by water. Many of Desmond's records were destroyed, which was a major blow, and he spent endless hours trying to contact his clients in an attempt to resurrect them. Several months passed before he was able to resume normal routines, and even then they were never quite normal.

When most of the Jewish refugees were released from internment, Desmond was caught up in the effort to find them homes and jobs, and, where possible, to set them up in business. He also continued to keep a close eye on the agricultural training centres he had helped to create.

As the head office of HHH was in Manchester, he also had to make frequent trips to the north in crowded trains along clogged tracks.

During his first three years with HHH, Desmond was only a junior partner and in going through the company's papers he discovered, almost by chance, that the scale of fees which Hesketh Hardy had purported to earn was wildly exaggerated and that he had been induced to acquire the partnership on extravagant terms. He therefore demanded that the terms be reviewed. When Hardy refused, he sued for misrepresentation. Such a case was almost unheard of. Moreover, Hardy was a friend of the family and there was pressure on Desmond from all sides to withdraw his suit. He was also warned that if the matter came before the courts it could ruin the whole partnership. There was, however, more than money involved. Desmond, usually the most affable of men, hated to be taken for a sucker. He also had a tenacious streak and once he embarked on a course, he rarely withdrew.

3

Building Up a Practice

———————

Though provincial by birth, Desmond had pronounced metropolitan tastes. He was disinclined to move to Manchester, even though some of his principal clients, including several major unions, were based there.

He may have felt that whatever the immediate advantages of Manchester, he had better prospects in London. Therefore, he acquired new offices in Norwich House, a fairly stately edifice of Portland stone, which he occupied until 1974 and which still stands at the corner of New Oxford Street and Southampton Place, Holborn. He was strategically well placed, on the fringe of the City on one side and on the fringe of the West End on the other. Over the years he attracted clients from both.

He rented first two, and then three floors of the building, which had long, dark corridors and high ceilings. Paintings adorned the panelled walls of his office as well as a large collection of originals from the work of the political cartoonist Ralph Sallon. He had two doors to his office, with direct access for major clients and indirect access, via his secretary Mrs Betty Arkell's office, for minor ones.

In later years callers might find a file on Clement Attlee or Harold Wilson lying casually on his desk, but in the early stages of his career his most prestigious client was the Dutch government-in-exile. As a Jewish accountant he also had his share of Jewish good causes – for example, the Council of Anglo-Jewish Preachers, the Cantor of the Dunstan Road Synagogue, Golders Green, the *Zionist Review* (a weekly publication with few readers and no money), and the Jewish Army Committee (whose efforts were eventually crowned with the creation of the Jewish Brigade in 1944), – all of whom kept him busy but none of whom made him rich. Indeed their demands on his time were sometimes in opposite ratio to their assets.

The number of his Jewish clients was due partly to his Zionist sympathies; partly to the fact that his offices were round the corner from those of the Zionist organisation, so that he was readily available for consultation; and partly to his friendship with Barnet Janner (later Lord Janner), a leading member of the Zionist movement, who in 1945 became Labour MP for north-west Leicester. 'Barney', as he was affectionately known in the Jewish community, later became President of the Board of Deputies of British Jews, on which Desmond also served for a time. 'Barney' tried to encourage him to assume a leading role in its affairs, but without success.

After the war, as the struggle for a Jewish state intensified, the life of the Jewish community was dominated by events in Palestine. The various organisations which had raised money for Zionist causes combined their efforts to form the Joint Palestine Appeal (later the Joint Israel Appeal), which was headed by the Marks and Spencer clan, Isaac Wolfson and other leading Jewish businessmen. Even men who before the war had thought of themselves as non-Zionists were caught up in the work of the JPA, and it is rather surprising that Desmond never held office either on the main board of the JPA or on any of its sub-committees. Nor, as he prospered, did he ever become a major contributor to its funds. He may have felt that he had done his bit for Zion through his work for the agricultural training scheme, and through his fund-raising activities. As we shall see, there was only one major Jewish organisation which consistently engaged his energies over the years.

Some of Desmond's commercial clients were fairly sizeable, but none was in the blue-chip class. They included a number of restaurants, some night-clubs, a bakery, a small cinema chain, hairdressers, furriers, dressmakers, cabinet-makers, glaziers, landlords and shopkeepers, the familiar small change of an accountancy practice. His most lucrative client, if not the largest, was his father-in-law, who had extensive property interests all over the Midlands and who headed a large cluster of small companies.

However, the clients who were to shape his future were the trade unions, a connection built up over many years by Hardy and enhanced by Desmond. They included railwaymen, print workers, the Durham area of the National Union of Miners, shop workers, the Post Office Union, the International Transport Workers' Union, and the Manor House Hospital in Golders Green (which was owned by the TUC). Their numbers increased when he became senior partner and included the electricians, the cinema workers and the Labour Party itself. By the end of the war he was recognised as the principal accountant and financial adviser to the Labour movement. He also became the financial adviser of several of the leading personalities in the movement, including Clement Attlee, Hugh Gaitskell and Sam Watson, secretary of the Durham miners, a major party figure with whom he enjoyed a particularly warm relationship.

There were occasional spasms of industrial unrest, especially in the mining areas, during the war, but in the main the unions, though growing in size, tended to be in a state of suspended animation. But once the fighting was over and young men flooded back into industry, the tempo and volume of Desmond's work increased.

In July 1945 Labour won a landslide victory in the general election. As accountant to the Party, Desmond advised on the financing of the election campaign and was drawn into its inner councils. However, the fact that he had close connections with the Party and the unions did not mean that he was in any way involved in formulating their policies. He might be asked by a union how much a strike would cost, but he would never be asked whether a strike should be held, or when it should be called off; and he would never, even on an informal basis, presume to offer his advice. He could come up with some original thoughts on practical matters, but was not, and never claimed to be an intellectual. He was an admired technocrat, but not a guru.

It is true that Desmond became a Labour supporter only after he became a partner in Hesketh Hardy. It is further true that he was ambitious and must have realised that as a middle-class Jew with no pedigree and limited means he had little hope of advancement through the Tory Party. His father had tried and failed to be elected as Mayor of Hendon. He could also not have failed to notice that while there were any number of Jewish Labour MPs in the House of Commons, there were only two Jewish Tories, both of them titled and rich. (This remained true right up to 1970, though things were to change after Edward Heath opened the Party to Jewish talent.) And finally, there was the all-important matter of contacts. He was on first-name terms with half the Labour front bench, but he only began to know prominent members of the Tory Party towards the end of his life and very few of them were to become members of his extensive social circle.

However, it was only after he began to work for the trade unions and was brought into touch with the harsh realities of working-class life that he began to see some of the limitations of free enterprise and to sympathise with the labour movement – although he did not subscribe to all its dogmas. In press interviews he liked to give the impression that he was apolitical, and the speeches he was later to make as a Labour peer suggested that he had serious reservations about Labour policies. But he did believe in the sort of moderate socialism preached by his mentor and guide Hugh Gaitskell.

As Brian Brivati explains in his recent biography of Gaitskell,*

For Gaitskell, democratic socialism had evolved to a point at which the tools existed to promote a more equal society through a combination of public ownership (in a wide variety of forms and decided upon a basis of efficiency); demand management (with an awareness of the disincentive effects of high taxation); and physical controls, either through indicative planning (national plans and targets) incentives or, if necessary, through directive measures (further nationalisation). These policies for equality were to be conducted through a mixed economy in which the 'capitalist' class had largely been replaced by the managerial class. It was to be implemented by a Labour Party that was a coalition of the political party and the trade union movement, which

* *Hugh Gaitskell* (Richard Cohen Books, 1996).

had long ago abandoned the transformatory or revolutionary road for gradualism and embraced the democratic
road. With the apparatus in place for changing society,
the tools of modern economic and social theory, and with
the labour movement united as a force for gaining,
through democratic means, the levers of power, society
would gradually improve as growth provided the
surpluses to spend on social welfare and greater equality.
The problems would be in finding the right kinds of
policy to implement – making the machine work – and
ensuring that the society created was ethically based but
also fun to live in.

Gaitskell's passionate belief in equality was as strong as his
faith that 'the Labour Party contained the people best able
to promote equality by the effective management of the
economy. . . . The society he sought was one in which the
individual was lifted out of poverty by opportunity.'

Self-interest may have brought Desmond into the Labour
Party, but mature reflection kept him there, though he may
have felt a little out of place as Labour lurched to the left in
the course of the 1960s and 1970s and disowned almost
everything that Gaitskell had stood for.

The Labour victory and the rise in the influence of the
Labour movement as a whole boosted his own standing and
that of his firm, and, in common with other members of his
profession, he benefited hugely from its fiscal policies.

During the war taxes had been pushed to confiscatory
levels and people accepted them glumly as part of the war
effort. After the war Labour reduced them slightly at the
bottom level but increased them at the very top. Super-tax
was 19/6 in the pound, while death duties on large estates
were raised to 75 per cent. As a result, both accountants and
lawyers were kept busy devising ingenious schemes for

avoiding the depredations of the Inland Revenue. Whenever one loophole was closed, they immediately set to discovering others.

While Desmond himself as yet had few clients in the top bracket, he nevertheless became an expert on the subject and produced a primer, 'The Avoidance and Evasion of Income Tax' (1945). Written with his customary clarity, it enjoyed a ready sale not only among accountants but also laymen. His clientele expanded in all directions. Unfortunately, although he was beginning to prosper professionally, his domestic situation was far less happy.

His wife would accompany him to the annual conferences of the Labour Party, the TUC and the various unions whose finances he handled, though, as she readily admits, she was bored out of her wits. 'We would come for a day or two but it felt like a month. Those dreadful hotels, those endless speeches.'

They separated in 1946 and divorce proceedings were finally completed on 19 May 1951. As a result, there was a sharp decline in his fee volume. He also had to repay a loan from his in-laws. He was always careful with money, but now he had to be particularly careful because he no longer had it. At thirty-six he was virtually starting again, and his circumstances were fairly bleak until he met Bronia. She believes that she brought not only brightness and hope into his life, but *mazel* (luck).

4

Bronia

Bronia at eighty-two still retains something of the good looks, the neat figure, the spirited personality and the Russian accent she had as a young woman – as well as a slight touch of mystery, which possibly derives from her accent and the wide range of her experience. She is multilingual, has been everywhere and knows everybody.

She was born in the Ukraine on 11 November 1915. Russia was at war and it was a time of hardship, danger and chaos. With the outbreak of the Revolution two years later, things became even more chaotic and dangerous. Marauding bands were everywhere and one no longer knew friend from foe. One went to bed to the sound of gun-fire not knowing if one would wake in the morning, and woke in the morning not knowing if one would survive the day. The family moved with great difficulty through one war zone after another to her mother's home in Tomaszow, Poland. 'God knows how we lived through it all,' her mother would tell her. 'God knows how we survived.' One reason for their survival was their inherent belief that God would see them through.

Things weren't easy in Tomaszow either, for Russia had hardly made peace with Germany before she was at war with Poland. The country was shaken by the thunder of guns and the depredations of marching armies. Bronia was too young to understand what was happening, but she was aware of the turmoil and the anxious faces around her. She was seven or eight before a semblance of peace and stability was restored, and even then the stability and the peace proved to be fairly precarious. As she later recalled, 'I was thirty before I really knew what it was to live in peace.' By then she was in England.

Both her parents, Josef and Rivka Eisen, were deeply devout and stemmed from dynasties of scholars, mystics and saints. The family name meant iron, and both in their different ways lived up to it. Her mother had lost two children in infancy and when she was pregnant with Bronia she was determined that she would survive. Another three daughters followed in quick succession, but her youngest child – a longed-for son – was ailing from birth. Fearing that he would die, she went on a hazardous journey by train to implore the Belzer Rebbe, leader of a small Hassidic sect, to pray for her son.

When she arrived at his house, there were crowds of people already there, so she slipped round to the kitchen entrance. When the Rebbe appeared, she fell at his feet. Taken aback, he asked who she was and, when told of her plight, he said that she must go home, where she would find her son recovering. He added that her son would live to be blessed at his wedding. (Bronia's brother remained weak, but later in Palestine, when he eventually got married, he did receive a blessing as the Rebbe had promised. He was also blessed with two children.)

Rivka was short, slight and very pretty, with large luminous eyes. As was usual among pious matrons, she shaved her head and wore a wig. Though in later years, by which time her hair was a silvery grey, she discarded the wig in favour of a bright kerchief. Bronia was in due course to acquire something of her mother's religiosity and all of her grim determination.

Josef, a tall, handsome, patriarchal figure, was trained as a rabbi, but never practised as one. At that time it was uncommon for girls in devout households to be given a religious education, but Josef made an exception of Bronia because for a number of years she represented the son he had hoped to have, and because she was the oldest and the brightest. After she returned from school in the afternoon, he would sit down with her to study Scripture, while the sounds of her sisters at play with their friends wafted in through the open windows. As she grew older, she had to attend *cheder* (religious school), and her father began to teach her the Talmud and the Halacha, the code of Jewish law:

A man should be aware of God's presence even in bed, and as soon as he wakes he should acknowledge the loving kindness of the Lord, blessed be he, for the soul, which was committed to Him faint and weary, was restored by Him renewed and refreshed, thus enabling man to serve God with devotion all day.

Bronia's day would begin and end with prayer. She was treated more like a son than a daughter; unlike her sisters, she did not have girlish toys and was discouraged from playing girlish games, or, indeed, games at all. Josef did, however, teach her chess, which in Poland was sacred to men, and she became a fairly adept player.

The family was prosperous, certainly by eastern European standards. Josef, for all his unworldly appearance and ways, was an enterprising businessman. Shortly after they settled in Tomaszow, he built up a substantial brick factory and also traded in timber, while her mother opened a gourmet food store piled high with delicacies which Bronia recalls as a sort of kosher Fortnum's.

They lived in a spacious home in a large square near the centre of town, shaded by lofty trees, and Bronia looks back on her early years with nostalgia. However, there were also moments of danger. Bronia recalls an incident that occurred when she was a small child after Russia invaded Poland. At the time Cossacks had started to attack the Jewish population and on one occasion two soldiers entered the square where her family lived, tied their horses to the pillars adorning the Eisens' house and looked around to see where to begin their assault. A Christian neighbour, who was a good friend to the Jews, deliberately lit a fire to attract the Cossacks to his home. There he gave them plenty of food and vodka, and succeeded in stopping them in their murderous pursuits. The local Jews, who had been sheltering in cellars and other hiding places, owed their lives to him.

The Eisens' week was dominated by the Sabbath and the year by the religious festivals, major and minor, with the patriarchal figure of her father reciting prayers, singing hymns and delivering homilies at one end of the table, her mother smiling at the other and the children ranged along either side.

Tomaszow was a sizeable town with a population of more than 30,000, of which about half was Jewish. It was a busy centre of commerce and the Eisens often had guests at their table – a business colleague, a visiting rabbi, an emissary from some seat of learning, who brought news from the wider world outside. The fare was abundant and delicious, for they had a splendid cook as well as cleaners, washers and laundry women. External events were menacing, but within their home, certainly on the Sabbath, they enjoyed an almost sublime sense of tranquillity. The children had a deep affection for their mother, but they approached their father with something like religious awe, as if he were God's representative on earth.

Many years later, when Bronia was already married to Desmond, she took Sam Watson, the Durham miners' leader, on a visit to her family in Tel Aviv. When her father entered the room, Bronia, her brother and her sisters – who by then were all in their forties – jumped to their feet. Watson was astonished. He had read of such respect for parents in Victorian novels, but had never come across it in real life.

Tomaszow was a fairly important centre of Jewish life with numerous synagogues, a strong Zionist organisation, its own weekly paper and a flourishing Jewish day school. Josef Eisen was a prominent and respected member of the community, but he was confident that he could give his daughters any Jewish education they might need and sent them instead to the local gymnasia, an elite high school, where Bronia showed early promise as a linguist (she speaks Russian, Polish, German, Hebrew and, of course, Yiddish).

As Bronia grew older, however, she found life in Tomaszow increasingly oppressive, which was possibly the price of her gymnasia education. She had been given an inkling of a wider world beyond the *shtetl* and a taste for European culture, which came into conflict with her traditional upbringing. And even though she may have been treated as an honorary male, she began to question the role accorded to females in traditional Jewish homes, as ancillaries to their mothers when single and as subservient to their husbands when married.

She was religious, and even today still enjoys some of the ancient traditions and ceremonies of Jewish life, but she could not conform to the example set by her mother or to the standards demanded by her father. She found that almost everything she did, or failed to do, was in breach of some ancient prohibition. 'You had to watch what you said, what you did, what you ate, what you wore, where you went and with whom you went. It was impossible.'

Then, when she was fifteen, an incident occurred which still brings tears to her eyes every time she describes it. It was a hot summer's afternoon – and summers in Poland can be very hot – and she and some friends decided to go swimming to a nearby lake. While splashing around in the water, they were joined by a number of boys, none of whom was Jewish. A passer-by happened to see them and rushed to tell her father the news. The ensuing scene settled the course of her life. Her father suddenly appeared from nowhere, his face white with fury like an avenging angel. As she emerged from the water, he slapped her across the face with such force that she fell to the ground and left her lying there in tears. She remembers the humiliation more than the pain and the confusion more than the humiliation, for she had always thought of her father as a kind and tolerant man. She determined there and then that, despite all the love and reverence she had for him and all the affection she had for her mother, she would have to leave home.

In common with most Jews in eastern Europe, she prayed daily for the return to Zion, but conditions in Poland in the early 1930s made it more than a pious sentiment. Anti-Semitism was rife and in school Bronia and her friends were often greeted with cries of 'Go to Palestine'. She was now determined to do just that.

Poland in the inter-war years was the heartland of the Zionist movement, and Bronia, together with many of her friends, was a member of Betar, the youth group of the right-wing Zionist Revisionist Party. Then, as if on cue,

1. Desmond as a young child

2. Strolling with his parents in the woods near Le Touquet

3. In holiday mood: Desmond's sense of fun never deserted him

4. With his sister Joan in the early 1930s

5. With his first love, Pimy Goldforb, in Davos

6. One of Desmond's many sketches of Pimy (front row) and others at the Davos Clinic

7. Desmond (extreme left), with Lord Melchett (centre), about to lead the Maccabi tennis team to Prague

8. Joseph and Rivka Eisen with their children, Poland 1922

9. Bronia in 1934

10. Bronia's son Frank

15. Ernest Bevin addresses a Labour Party Conference with Hugh Dalton (left) and Herbert Morrison looking on. Desmond always enjoyed attending Conference in his role as financial adviser

16 and 17. In his attempts to encourage Labour and Capital to work together, Desmond forged close links with many Union leaders. Here he is seen with Frank Cousins on the deck of the *SS Theodor Herzl* in 1957 and with Danny McGarvey General Secretary of the Boilermakers' Union

18. Clement Attlee and Hugh Gaitskell, 1962. Desmond and Bronia got to know both Labour leaders and their families well

19. The annual Durham Miners' Gala was a favourite event with both Desmond and Bronia and an enjoyable social gathering for their political friends and colleagues: Sam Watson (far left), leader of the Durham miners, Frank Cousins, Hugh and Dora Gaitskell and Lady Summerskill

20. Desmond joins Harold Wilson, George Brown and Tony Benn to watch the Miners' Gala from the balcony of the Royal County Hotel

21. Deep in conversation with trade union leader Vic Feather

22. With Israeli Prime Minister Golda Meir in London

23. With Indira Gandhi in Calcutta

24. Greeting Her Majesty Queen Elizabeth in her role as patron of Norwood. Lord Samuel the ex-President of Norwood, is in the background

Vladimir Jabotinsky, founder of the Party and one of the foremost orators of his day, came to address the Jewish community in Tomaszow. His insistence that there was no future for Jews in Poland put the seal on her plans.

She neglected her lessons and spent more and more of her time in Betar She filled her room with Zionist posters and could hardly talk about anything except Betar, Jabotinsky and Palestine. Her parents, though troubled by her behaviour, were confident that she would see sense as she grew older. They didn't know their own daughter. She grew more determined with every passing month, and they finally relented. They would let her go to Palestine, but not on her own.

First she went to Warsaw with a cousin, because at that time one couldn't travel alone in Poland under the age of twenty-one. Betar was familiar with her situation and had established procedures to cope with it. At Jabotinsky's office in Warsaw, where many young men and women were helping to process applications to go to Palestine, they introduced her to Leslie (Chaim) Kaufman, a rabbi's son who was equally anxious to settle in Palestine. In 1933 she therefore entered into what she called 'a marriage of convenience'. She was eighteen and he was twenty-four. Her father, whom she had summoned from Tomaszow and who was delighted by the match, even gave her a small dowry. For 'a marriage of convenience' it was curiously long lived.

Bronia had been warned that life in Palestine would be harsh, but nothing quite prepared her for the hardships they actually had to face: the fierce heat, the mosquitoes, the endless toil, the meagre fare, the primitive accommodation and the political commotion. 'We worked in the orange groves from dawn till dusk and by the time we got back we were too weary to eat – not that there was all that much worth eating. Oranges, of course, dry bread, a few olives, a bit of cheese. All those films they used to show about *chalutzim* [workers] dancing and singing round a camp-fire made me laugh. I was far too exhausted for that and collapsed on a pile of rags I called a bed, but I got used to it.' The trouble was that she never quite got used to her husband. And much as she loved Palestine itself, she looks back on those years as amongst the darkest in her life.

Her stay did, however, have one positive result. As the years passed anti-Semitism in Poland became more virulent and life for Polish Jewry more oppressive. After prolonged deliberation, her family finally decided to pull up roots and join her in Palestine. By then there were considerable restrictions on immigration, and were it not for the fact that they already had a daughter in the country, they might never have received the necessary permits. She draws great comfort from the thought that in settling in Palestine she may have saved the lives of her parents and siblings.

By the time they arrived, however, a further addition to the family was on the way. Bronia was pregnant. What she still insists on calling 'a marriage of convenience' had proved to be singularly inconvenient. Her son Frank was born in June 1936.

In 1937 Kaufman left Bronia in Palestine and moved to London, where his parents had set up a wine business. Two years later, after not having heard from her husband or receiving any money from him to help support their son, Bronia decided to follow him to London with the intention of getting a divorce.

When she arrived, she was met at Victoria Station by her parents-in-law, whom she introduced to her son for the first time. Her husband, who had by now joined the Merchant Navy, was not around. She stayed with her parents-in-law for about six months and then found a four-bedroomed flat above a shop in Hendon, which she was able to rent with the small sum of money that her father sent her regularly.

Unfortunately, this financial help ceased during the war because of difficulties transferring the money from Palestine. Instead, she was forced to rent out one of her rooms to a German couple.

Divorce proceedings were protracted and she finally received a divorce in 1947 on the grounds of Kaufman's adultery. He paid her a lump sum of £2,500, alimony of about £3 per week and undertook to pay his son's school fees and expenses. However, he rarely took the trouble to see his son. When it comes to her first marriage, Bronia obviously regards it as one of the great mistakes of her life, wishes it had never happened and, were it not for the fact that she had a son, she might have erased it from her memory altogether.

In the meantime she was in no hurry to return to Tel Aviv. Life in the Blitz had given her a sense of kinship with Londoners and she had been able to travel a little. As a result, she had grown to love and admire the country. She took out naturalisation papers and in 1948 became a British subject, thanks to the magistrate of the Tel Aviv courts who had helped her all the way.

Post-war England may have seemed a bleak place to others, but it did not seem so to her. It was stable, peaceful and unhurried, and though she suffered loneliness, penury and hardship, it gave her a sense of tranquillity she had experienced in neither Poland nor Palestine. Frank, who had been evacuated for a short time during the war, was now at Whitinghame College, a Jewish boarding-school in Brighton, where he was fairly happy. Bronia was therefore able to attend evening classes to improve her English and her understanding of literature and art. And fond though she was of her parents, she had left home to escape their strictness at eighteen and had no wish to return to it at thirty.

She was a very attractive young woman and turned heads

wherever she went, but denies absolutely that she had formed any sort of romantic attachment which might have kept her in London. She had found a new life, was in no hurry to change it and was beginning to reconcile herself to the thought that she would probably not marry again.

While in London she was visited by her younger sister Livia, who remained with her for over a year. Livia, who was tall, lively and attractive, had acquired some acting experience in Tel Aviv and hoped to become a film star. She circulated her photographs amongst various agencies and eventually obtained an introduction to Sir Alexander Korda. Bronia went along to keep her company, or rather to act as chaperone, but it did not lead to a screen part or even a screen test.

'All your fault,' she told Bronia later. 'If I'd gone on my own, he'd have chased me round the room and I'd have got a part.'

'What sort of part,' Bronia replied, 'and at what price?'

Livia took lessons in voice production to eliminate her foreign accent and eventually met another producer, who gave her a part in *The Farmer's Wife*, a rustic comedy based on the novel by Eden Phillpotts. She had a few lines which she uttered with aplomb, but with her flashing eyes and exotic appearance did not quite look the part of a country wench, and it did not lead to anything better. She returned to Tel Aviv, and in 1948, when El Al Airlines was set up, she became Israel's first air-hostess and featured prominently in its advertising campaigns. She later married a rabbi.

Bronia's own situation, in the meantime, was rather more prosaic. She still lived in the flat in Hendon, but the tiny sum she received by way of alimony was not enough to make ends meet. Her father sent her the occasional cheque and she also kept a lodger, which made things slightly easier, and the picture she paints of her life is one of cheerful privation. Food was still strictly rationed, though the war was over, and she recalls that she couldn't always afford her full meat ration and would pick up a few bones from the butcher to make soup.

She describes herself as something of a recluse, though she had a number of friends including Oscar and Bela Cantor, who lived in Swiss Cottage. Oscar was a citrus importer who had business dealings with her father, who by the outbreak of war had acquired a number of orange groves.

Bela often complained that for a young woman Bronia was being a little too reclusive for her own good and would take her along to various social events at the nearby Hampstead Synagogue. Bronia accompanied her with some reluctance. She had by then virtually abandoned her Judaism and no longer felt at ease in synagogal surroundings for they evoked too much of a past she was anxious to forget. Nor was she entirely happy in the company of English Jews, whom she found too light-hearted, too frivolous and too chatty. She was never tongue-tied when she had something to say, but could not understand the compulsion of people to make conversation when they had nothing to say and was not yet adept at small-talk. She was also deeply conscious of the fact that she was not as well dressed as the women around her. 'The new look' with longer skirts had just come into vogue, and she was decidedly 'old look'.

Then one evening towards the end of 1948 Bela took her to a reception to mark the end of the Jewish festival of Simchat Torah. It was there that she met Desmond. Though she didn't know it at the time, the encounter was to transform her life – and his.

5

Courtship and Marriage

Desmond was attractive, attentive and charming, and a few days later he phoned Mrs Cantor to ask if he could take her protégée out to lunch. Protocol required such niceties in those days, and Desmond was a stickler for protocol.

Lunch was a novel experience for Bronia, for she rarely ate any, and Desmond took her to Ciro's, one of the most exclusive restaurants in London. She was slightly overwhelmed. Ciro, with its ritzy interior and elegant clientele, was not quite her scene, nor, indeed, was the West End itself. She wasn't sure what to order or how, or what to drink, or whether to drink at all. She was also slightly overwhelmed by Desmond, his build, his size, his air of prosperity and authority, and the way the waiters danced around him as if he owned the place. He was a man about town, whereas she wasn't even a woman around the suburbs. He did seem a little full of himself but his relaxed, amiable manner soon put her at ease.

He was light-hearted, witty, made some complimentary remarks about her appearance and dress, asked her a little about herself, spoke about his work and the events of the day, dropped some famous names, but otherwise said little about himself. It was left to Mrs Cantor to tell her that he was married, but that he was separated from his wife 'and lives alone pending a divorce'.

Then one evening he phoned to invite her to a charity dinner and ball at the Grosvenor House Hotel. The invitation threw her into a panic. It was not merely that charity dinners were outside her experience and that she had never been to a ball in her life, but that she had nothing to wear. She didn't even have an un-scuffed handbag.

Bela Cantor bought her a pair of satin shoes with a matching handbag and some black satin curtain material, which her dressmaker fashioned into a dress. As she had no jewellery, the dressmaker added shoulder straps made of glittering rhinestones, which shimmered like diamonds. It might have looked cheap or even frumpish on anyone else; on Bronia it looked stylish and elegant.

Desmond, who was involved in running the whole event, had also thoughtfully provided her with an escort, a tall, mysterious but striking figure called Julian Du Park, who presented himself at the door of her tiny flat wearing a black cape lined with scarlet and a monocle in his eye. Bronia was startled and wondered for a moment if she wasn't being taken to a fancy-dress ball.

She arrived in something of a daze, feeling strange and out of place. She sipped a glass of wine to steady herself and only relaxed after she was introduced to Desmond's mother. They struck up an immediate rapport.

Lily Hirshfield was a large, hearty Englishwoman, with smiling features, blue eyes and a loud voice, while Bronia – as she describes herself at this time – was small, subdued, demure, something of a waif. Perhaps her very demureness appealed to Lily. Bronia was decidedly pretty, but looked like a woman who had been through hard times.

As a woman of means, Desmond's first wife had had to attend a great many charity functions and was understandably blasé about them. Bronia on the other hand was excited, like a young girl at her first ball, which indeed it was. Her foreign accent and continental air also added a slightly exotic touch to her personality.

'I like her,' said Lily to her husband. 'I like her very much. Just the girl for Desmond.'

Desmond's marriage had already broken down by the time they met, and her ready acceptance by his mother gave it the *coup de grâce*.

They met fairly regularly after that, either at Sunday lunch with the Cantors or in his parents' house, or for long walks across Hampstead Heath. Desmond told her candidly that his first marriage had been arranged and influenced by family pressures, and that he had launched divorce proceedings. He wanted to make a new start. Yet when he formally proposed at the end of 1950, it came as something of a shock. They had known each other for two years by then, but she felt that she was being rushed.

She was happy in his company and admired everything about him – except, possibly, his growing girth – but she was too seared by memories of her first marriage to rush readily into another. She wanted time to think and, at Desmond's suggestion, she flew to Tel Aviv to discuss the matter with her family.

She was away for six weeks and during that time he wrote to her daily, sometimes twice a day, long, affectionate letters written mostly in the small hours of the night. The following letter was fairly typical:

My Dearest Darling Precious Angel,

I'm full up as I write – full of deep feelings and reminiscences and in a mood for pouring out my thoughts in a way which happens to me rarely. So being in a mood for writing at this moment this looks like being something of a booklet – or should I rather say a token of my love and affection for you.

It is often said, proverbially, that 'absence makes the heart grow fonder'. Well if it is possible for me to be fonder of you tonight – just twenty-four hours after your departure – than this time last night – I would say I'm fonder. In fact I'm no more fond but a good deal clearer in mind and outlook. In these past awful hours I've felt as I've never felt before but I see the future bright and vivid before me.

His letters were ineloquent, and the succession of affecionate terms, each piled on top of the other, may seem excessive, but their very ineloquence suggests an uncontrolled rush of feeling. They didn't quite go with the light-hearted man she had come to know and were something of a revelation, albeit a welcome one. His shyness about displaying his emotions won her over.

She returned to London at the end of April and Desmond met her at the airport with a vast bouquet of flowers and a tiny card, which read: 'To welcome home at long last my sweet and precious darling angel – with the deepest love there could be. From your soon to be P.G. Devoted and ever loving husband. Desmond.' 'P.G.' stands for 'Please God', an expression devout Jews use when touching on the future. Desmond was not that devout, but he was deeply superstitious.

Bronia brought him two good-luck charms, which he wore round his neck on a gold chain to the end of his days, and which she still retains. One was made up of the Hebrew word *'chai'*, meaning life, and the other *'mazel'*, meaning good luck. To these he added a third with the image of the god Thor, a thoroughly pagan deity, but then, as a good accountant, he was always careful to hedge his bets.

Three months later, on 19 July 1951, they were married in a small ceremony at St John's Wood Liberal Synagogue in the presence of a handful of friends. There was no one there from her family and few members from his, and the whole event was strangely reminiscent of his father's wedding ceremony in the Bradford Reform Synagogue some forty years earlier.

They chose the Liberal Synagogue because Desmond had received a civil divorce but not a religious one, so that according to Jewish Law he was still married. The fact was a source of some distress to Bronia's father and out of concern for his feelings Desmond eventually obtained a *get* (a religious divorce).

They began married life in the small bachelor flat which Desmond occupied in Curzon Street. They were exceedingly happy. Desmond had always been well looked after, so he had never learned to look after himself. He could make himself a cup of tea, if necessary, but didn't even know how to boil an egg. After a long day in the office, he would usually eat out at an expensive restaurant, sometimes in company, often on his own. Though his existence was far from cheerless, he was never quite the hearty, debonair man about town he looked. He loved orderliness and stability and yearned for the care and affection of a loving wife. Bronia provided everything he could have hoped for.

She speaks of Desmond as her first love, her last love and her only love, and a letter she sent him two years after their wedding, while she was visiting her parents in Tel Aviv, conveys the force of her emotions:

To my Dearest Darling:

With all loving wishes on this day of our anniversary. May our future be a long, lasting happy one. With a gentle love like an early sun of a summer morning that caresses the early morning mist away. Together may we look to a happy future, with love and contentment, good health and everything that goes with it.

To my wonderful husband – from your very dear wife.

Desmond replied in similar terms:

My sweetheart Darling, I cannot wait to see you – when are you coming home? Have you reserved your seat yet? God willing may we please God be united more completely and utterly than we are now. Darling, do you want to marry in London or in Israel? Please discuss everything completely with your dear parents before you come home.

They married again in 1954 at a religious ceremony in Tel Aviv. It was only then that Desmond was accepted as a full member of her family.

At this stage in their fortunes they were not particularly well off, and, a little improbably for an accountant who should have known how far the odds were stacked against him, Desmond hoped to make a killing through the football pools. He encouraged Bronia to do the same, as one may see from a further paragraph in the same letter: 'Walked down Piccadilly – got the evening papers with football results and came straight back here to check the pools. No luck – but very near indeed again. Your coupon was the best.' On one occasion Desmond's office syndicate won and Desmond, whose share was £700 – a substantial sum in those days – went out and bought Bronia a fur evening cape with a large part of his winnings.

The following year they moved into a seven-roomed apartment in Hanover Gate Mansions, near Baker Street. Like many mansion flats in London, the block had a fairly nondescript, even drab façade and had been 'run up' during the great building boom of the 1930s. However, their flat was spacious and conveniently situated with Regent's Park over the road and the Cricket Club at Lord's round the corner. Bronia quickly imposed her own personality on it, so that it acquired the elegance and atmosphere of a French salon.

They would visit Israel at least once a year and Desmond soon felt a great affection for Bronia's parents. They, for their part, came to regard him as a cherished son. Her father adopted the curious habit of sending Desmond a handful of gold Russian roubles on his birthday, which he kept as a sort of talisman. Each, however, was not quite certain what to make of the other, for they lived in different worlds, the father bearded and patriarchal like a figure out of the Old Testament, Desmond like someone out of a Regency novel, the one steeped in mysticism and Jewish tradition, the other a man of the world revelling in worldly pleasures; but each viewed the other with the greatest respect.

Professor Alexander Russell, a paediatrician with whom Desmond was working on plans for a Jerusalem children's home in the early 1970s, once visited the Eisens with Desmond and still retains vivid memories of the occasion: 'The old man, a striking figure with glowing features and a long white beard, reminded me of the Prophet Elijah. He couldn't speak English, Desmond couldn't speak Yiddish, and they got by in German, but they were not like two members of a family chatting with one another. Desmond was not completely at ease in his presence and addressed him with great deference, like a pupil addressing his master. I'd never known him to be like that. It was all rather touching.'

Desmond was particularly devoted to his mother-in-law. They did not find it easy to communicate, for they too had a language problem, and Bronia would act as an interpreter, but there was no need to translate their mutual affection into words.

During one visit Desmond was told that the Eisens had had some difficulty in getting a new phone installed. He loved to be of service. He also loved to show what influence he could exercise, and this was an ideal occasion for a display of both. He promptly phoned his friend Shimon Peres, who happened to be Minister of Communications at the time, and they got a new line within days.

Desmond's and Bronia's home from home in Israel was the Tel Aviv Hilton, where they frequently entertained her parents. Unfortunately, they were never able to entertain them in London. Desmond wrote to Bronia on one occasion: 'Oh, how I wish they would come over here and stay in our flat for a month or so,' but his wish was never fulfilled. Space was no problem, but the catering arrangements were. Whenever Bronia's parents came to a meal at the Hilton – which was strictly kosher – her father would insist on examining the kitchen to make sure that it was kosher enough for his exacting standards. He would have found it impossible to eat in their London home; even though there were any number of good kosher caterers who would have been delighted to meet his needs.

The real problem lay in the appearance and personality of Bronia's father, for with his small white beard, large black skull-cap and deep religiosity, he would have been a forceful reminder of the traditions and usages they had discarded. He never travelled without his prayer-shawl, phylacteries and a case full of devotional books, and he would almost have converted their elegant home – a meeting place of England's political elite – into a synagogue. Desmond and

Bronia's kingdom was of this world, whereas Eisen's was of the next. He would never have dreamt of commenting on their lifestyle, but they would have sensed his disapproval. He would have cramped their style.

Desmond had never tried to hide his Jewishness. Indeed, as he made clear in more than one speech in the House of Lords, he was proud of it, but he never cared to flaunt it and having Eisen around would have been a bit like flaunting it. Desmond was a Jew in mufti, whereas Eisen gloried in the full panoply of the faith. Though he was not a fanatic, he was too Jewish by half, too pious, too much a relic of the past. And to Bronia he represented a startling reminder of fraught circumstances and fraught lives, and how far she had strayed from her early upbringing.

When her mother died after a long illness in 1968, Bronia was by her bedside. Desmond, alone in London, was overwhelmed by the news:

> . . . I shall miss her very much – always. And as long as I live I shall recall her sweetness, and her fine traditional Jewish character. I held her in very great affection, as you know, and I always knew she had the same affection for me, which I cherished.
>
> Darling, I know all of you have lost a cherished mother and that your grief is tremendous and must seem irreparable in these awful days. But, my sweetheart, please try if you can to understand that God has granted your Darling mother a truly merciful release from her pain and suffering. She has hurried on from the physical torments of the last weeks, and the associations of this earth – to her rightful place in heaven. I believe she will continue to watch over you and all her Dear ones so long as you live. Through her greatness, her kindness and her fond affection, her honesty and her uprightness, she will

be a constant and wonderful memory to us all, she will guide us in our way through life – and the Almighty God will rest her Dear soul in Peace.

It was a spontaneous outburst of emotion, which not only showed the depth of his feelings for Bronia's mother but his basic religiosity. When he spoke of 'her rightful place in heaven', he was not merely using a metaphor but indicating his faith in the hereafter and the immortality of the soul. He may have ceased to be an observant Jew, but he was still a believing one.

The same letter also gave eloquent expression to his feelings about Bronia's father:

> ... that truly wonderful, glorious, great and wise man ... my heart goes out to him in his hour of deep sorrow – his loss is so great!
>
> I pray Darling that you do for your Dearest Father – all of you whatever you can. Stay by him, comfort him, keep at his side while he mourns and while he frets. Help him through his nightmare to pleasanter days beyond. God will surely give strength and courage to one of his finest sons in the hour of need. . . .

Josef Eisen, sustained by his faith, treated his bereavement stoically. However, they were a devoted pair and after his wife's death he went into a decline. He eventually died in 1975.

Bronia had, of course, kept her parents regularly informed of Desmond's progress in life, his elevation to the peerage, his speeches in the Lords. They took immense pride in his achievements, but they never saw him in his scarlet and ermine when he took his seat in the House, or during the State Opening of Parliament, or even in the splendid surroundings of their own home. 'They never hinted that they wanted to come,' says Bronia. 'I never suggested that they should come, and that's how it was.' She has regrets on the matter to this day.

Her relationship with Desmond's parents, on the other hand, was happy and uncomplicated, if only because they lived in the same world – more or less – and had much the same values. She loved and admired Lily's good looks, high spirits, warm temperament and theatrical manner, a 'Yiddisher' mamma without 'Yiddisher' hang-ups.

Leo, though lively, amiable and hearty, with a ready fund of pleasantries, was almost dour compared to his wife. Desmond and Bronia would visit them at least once a week, usually on a Sunday, either in Hendon or, after they retired to the country, in Esher. They were often joined by Desmond's sister Joan, with whom he was on particularly close terms, and who lived nearby in Weybridge. She had married Eric Rubenstein, a successful solicitor, and had two daughters, Jane and Anne, whom she sometimes brought with her. Desmond took great pleasure in their company and would question them closely on their progress at school, while Leo surveyed them all with a look of unalloyed joy. He may not have got very far in life himself, but he had not done badly through his progeny.

Leo died suddenly while on holiday in Cannes on New Year's Day 1966. After his body was embalmed and flown to London in a zinc coffin, he was buried at Bushey cemetery some six days later.

In his will he left Lily £11,000 and expressed 'the sincere hope that after my death my children will remain staunch friends and will help one another to their fullest extent and will remain united together in honour of their parents'. The very language he used suggested that he may have had apprehensions on the matter, which in the event were not misplaced, for while the brothers were devoted to their younger sister, they did not always get on well with one another. Joan and her husband did their best to neutralise the differences which had arisen between them, and Lily urged them to 'never quarrel' and to 'always look after one another if needed'.

Lily, who was seventy-four when Leo died, did not adapt readily to widowhood or old age. She moved into a small flat in Marble Arch, but liked to have company and commotion around her and spent much of her time, smartly attired and coiffed, drinking coffee in the lounge of the Cumberland Hotel, which was almost next door. One afternoon she found herself in conversation with a prosperous Greek farmer, a man in his eighties. They became friends and he invited her to visit him in Greece. The few thousand pounds Leo had left her did not allow her to live in the manner to which she felt entitled and she was helped out by her children, but when she told them that she wanted to fly to Greece, and why, they were unwilling to finance what sounded like an escapade. Lily, however, was not prepared to be treated like a child by her own children. She sold some crystal glasses and a trinket or two and off she went. Her new friend greeted her warmly on arrival and installed her in a luxury hotel, but at the end of her stay she found that she had to pay the bill and had to pawn some of her jewellery before she could leave.

The incident did not impair their relationship and when he was next in London, she entertained him and some of his friends at the Caprice, one of the most expensive restaurants in London. This meant the sale of more crystal glasses and a few bits of family silver. When the Greek vanished from the scene, she made other friends and entertained them in equally expensive surroundings, and sold off a few more trinkets and even odd pieces of furniture. Her flat, though small, was becoming bare.

Bronia was deputed to talk to her, woman to woman, and tried to explain that she was in danger of being exploited, as women of a certain age often were. Lily listened to her with impatience and even resentment and dismissed such fears. She had her own life, her own way of doing things and knew how to look after herself, and she continued to find new friends and admirers until she was well into her eighties. She was becoming a source of consternation, but Bronia could not help but admire her style, her poise and her determination not to retreat into the shadows. She died in 1978, a trouper to the last.

6

Entertaining Labour

From the moment Bronia married Desmond, she was convinced that fate had prepared her for the role, not only of wife but of partner in a historic enterprise, and that he was not only her husband but a man of destiny.

He had style and class, and looked like a natural leader of men, and she always put great store by appearance. To Bronia, looks, certainly in the case of Desmond, represented an outer expression of inner grace, and she is still surrounded by portraits of him in oil, sketches, photographs and cartoons, as if to reassure herself that he was not a figment of her imagination.

But Desmond was not just handsome. He had obvious ability, important connections and was on first-name terms with the Prime Minister and half the Cabinet. He had been kept back hitherto by what she thought of as an unfortunate, even a disastrous, marriage and his natural diffidence, but with her at his side she was confident that he would finally take off.

With the devastation of the war behind them, and a brave new world ahead, the timing seemed propitious. He was thirty-eight and she was thirty-five, which was not too late for a new start. Even so, there was no time to be lost.

The picture she paints of herself in the pre-Desmond years as a shy, impoverished recluse is unconvincing. if only because of the elegant, glittering, self-assured hostess she soon became. It is possible that her marriage to Desmond gave her confidence, but one suspects that she was born with it. Once they moved into Hanover Gate Mansions, she made it not only into a home but a stage on which Desmond could display his talents as a *bon vivant*, raconteur, man of affairs and host. At same time, while proud of her husband, she was at pains to insist that she was someone in her own right and no mere helpmeet. She preferred to be addressed as Bronia – short for Broniaslova – Hirshfield rather than Mrs Desmond Hirshfield.

Bronia did not organise his life – that he was perfectly capable of doing himself with help from his secretary – but she believes that she raised his horizons and redressed his diffidence with her drive. Although he was already a successful accountant, on the board of management of his local synagogue, a trustee of various Jewish charities and something of a public figure in Jewish life, she felt that he was made for higher things. She therefore converted their home into a political salon, charmed her way into the higher echelons of the Labour Party and helped to propel him to national prominence. He even changed in appearance. From weighing sixteen stone with the plump, well-fed look of a man who slept at night, he slimmed down to almost thirteen stone.

Though she was the daughter of business people with a sharp business mind of her own, she never attempted to

interfere in his business or professional life. She only offered
help and advice on such matters when asked, but was
always there whenever Desmond needed her. The fact that
they had no children meant that she could devote herself to
him and excel in the roles of wife, mistress, mentor and
companion.

Labour's defeat in the 1951 elections may have been
something of a setback to Desmond, but the Conservative
victory brought an end to rationing and was followed by the
gradual elimination of shortages. A touch of colour began
to brighten the horizon and the years of austerity were over.
The good things of life were again available if one had the
money. Hostesses again had the opportunity to shine, and
few Labour hostesses shone quite as brightly as Bronia.

She was immensely painstaking. She enrolled in a cordon
bleu cookery class and took a course in interior decorating.
At the same time, she and Desmond haunted sales rooms,
country-house auctions and antique shops to bring together
the sort of furniture, furnishings and pictures they wanted
for their flat. They were both perfectionists so that the
process was never quite complete, and Bronia – sometimes
to his mild irritation, and occasionally to his grave displeasure – kept adding new items and disposing of old ones for
as long as he lived. Their home became stylish and comfortable, even cosy.

Bronia was particularly proud of her dining-room, which
was high-ceilinged and spacious, with a huge Empire mirror
covering an entire wall at one end, a Victorian ormolu
chandelier overhanging the centre, and twelve large
Regency chairs. The dining-room opened on to a fully
equipped bar, and beyond the bar there was a sitting-room
with a pair of chesterfield sofas and easy chairs. There was
also a book-lined study, so that when guests wanted to
escape from the general throng for a quiet *tête-à-tête*, or

73

even a quiet read, they had ample space to do so.

Much of the flat was lined with pictures, none of which was particularly expensive. Some of them looked like old masters, including one from what Bronia describes as 'the school of Caravaggio', and another from that of Goya; there were also several French paintings, works by various artists they had befriended and a number of landscapes painted by Desmond.

They also helped to launch a number of artists, one of whom was a Durham miner called McGuinness. They brought him south and organised an exhibition for him at a Mayfair gallery. It was a sell-out.

The others included two Maltese brothers, Willy and Winston Apap, the one a painter, the other a sculptor, whose work was brought to their attention by Lord Mountbatten during a visit to Valletta. Bronia was particularly impressed with them both. She brought them to London, moved all her furniture into a depository, converted her flat into a gallery, laid on a lavish reception which would have sufficed for a wedding breakfast and invited all her rich friends. By the end of the day every picture was sold.

The brothers also received commissions for innumerable portraits. Bronia commissioned one of herself and another of Desmond. The one of herself painted when she was in her fifties shows a very attractive woman, slim, well-preserved, winsome, wilful, mischievous and formidable. The one of Desmond, on the other hand, in black jacket and striped trousers, suggests authority and success, the quiet satisfaction of the man who has made it. It is Desmond at his zenith.

The apartment was rather splendid and comfortable, but nothing in the château quite matched the châtelaine, small, sparkling, greeting one guest, kissing another, making each one feel that the occasion was being staged for his particular benefit. She may have been new to society, but she acted as if she had been born to the role. She had a natural dress sense and, although she had left Poland in her teens, she had inherited from her mother a touch of continental chic.

Desmond, warm and welcoming with a pipe in one hand and a glass in the other, could give a sense of occasion to a gathering by his very presence. 'He was such a very remarkable man,' said Lady Longford, who became a close family friend; 'a superb host, a charmer. The room lit up when he appeared.' He knew a lot about wine, but, like most Jews of his class, was rather more interested in food. He liked a scotch, but was too mindful of his responsibilities to have more than a glass or two. They usually entertained on two evenings a week and occasionally at lunchtime on Sundays. In the evenings they would have about a dozen guests round the dinner table. On Sundays they served a buffet lunch on the verandah. This was a less formal gathering and there would sometimes be as many as fifty guests.

Anne Sebba, Joan's daughter, who was to become a distinguished biographer, has happy memories of these Sunday lunches: 'I always looked forward to them. Crowds of people, famous names, famous faces, always someone interesting to talk to. It was exciting even to eavesdrop. For a young girl like me it was an education.'

They also gave eve-of-election parties, with the constant arrival of journalists, friends and politicians, the television on and drinks served through the night.

Their reputation for hospitality was such that Hanover Gate Mansions came to be thought of among some trade unionists and Labour MPs as an after-hours drinking club. Their flat was on the first floor overlooking a trunk road to the north, and if their lights were on, MPs might drop by for a nightcap after a late-night sitting. On occasion they might drop by even when the lights were off, often throwing stones at the window to attract Desmond's attention. Bronia would greet them in her house-coat and they would quite happily sit around chatting until the early hours of the morning.

There were many Desmonds: the political Desmond, Desmond the accountant, the synagogue Desmond, Desmond the artist and art-lover, and Desmond the uncle and family man, each of whom tended to attract a different group of people He and Bronia kept the different groups in different compartments, though a dinner for politicians might include a leavening of journalists and artists, and a gathering of industrialists and businessmen might include a few trade unionists and lawyers.

Their home, however, was principally a gathering place for the left and sometimes guests would break out into a spirited rendering of 'We'll keep the Red Flag flying here'. Richard Crossman, who was not a regular guest, did not quite know what to make of his host and referred to him in his memoirs as 'the mysterious Desmond Hirshfield'. His mystification, however, was not entirely surprising, for Desmond had an influence in the Party without holding any actual office or enjoying any particular prominence in the country at large; he was not even particularly rich.

Geoffrey Goodman, a prominent Fleet Street Labour journalist, said of the dinners: 'Good food, splendid wine, informed company and delicious gossip. Good place to pick up a good story, unattributable, of course, but very useful.'

The general atmosphere of the place was nicely summed up in a letter to Bronia from Nance Cousins, the wife of the prominent trade union leader Frank Cousins:

Thank you for last night as well as all the other nights we had with you. I hope you enjoyed it as much as we did.

Actually you did a service to our movement because Frank and Nye [Bevan] ought to see one another much more often, not just in committee and such, but like last night, where they were relaxed and themselves. I've always felt they could do big things together.

Bronia's first cook was Irish, an amiable woman and an excellent cook, but her previous employer had been Jewish and she had come to specialise in traditional Jewish fare. Bronia wanted something more cosmopolitan and found herself another cook. She arranged everything with the greatest care and kept an index to make sure that the same guest was not confronted with the same people at successive parties, or even with the same dishes. The result was rarely less than perfect.

Susan Soskice, wife of the Labour peer Lord Soskice, wrote to her after one meal: 'Just a note to thank you and Desmond for the simply lovely dinner party last night. Frank and I enjoyed it immensely. The table as usual looked so beautiful, and the food was delicious. What a clever girl you are! You were looking lovely.' No woman is on oath when writing a letter of thanks for hospitality received, but an invitation to Hanover Gate Mansions acquired a social cachet among both socialists and socialites.

Bronia and Desmond took immense pains with the seating plans and left nothing to chance. They sent out invitations well in advance so that in the event of refusals they could come up with other likely names. Even then they were sometimes let down at the last minute and in later years Bronia adopted the habit of sending out reminders. 'You had to have the right social mix and know all the gossip,' she says, 'because there were some people you couldn't have under the same roof at the same time, and certainly not round the same table.'

She recalls a disastrous evening when there was a violent

confrontation between Nye Bevan and Frank Cousins. George Brown, on the other hand, could sometimes even attack his friends. On one occasion he turned on Alma Birk – who later, as Baroness Birk, was to become a prominent Labour peer – over something she had written in the *New Statesman* and berated her at the top of his voice for some minutes. 'He was good fun but completely unpredictable,' said Bronia, 'but then he may have been good fun because he was unpredictable.' Desmond took an unashamed delight in the occasional fracas. It was as good as a floor-show and made for a memorable evening.

Such scenes, however, were rare and Hanover Gate Mansions was usually a venue for serious political discussions where everyone felt sufficiently at ease to speak freely and, sometimes, indiscreetly.

Hugh Gaitskell recalled in his diary an evening with the Hirshfields in 1954. He was delayed and he and his wife only turned up after eleven o'clock. The party was still going strong and the company included Sam Watson, head of the Durham miners. Attlee was still Leader of the Labour Party, but everyone expected him to step down in the near future. Both Bevan and Gaitskell hoped to succeed him and were frantically jockeying for position. Watson and the Durham miners were among Gaitskell's keenest supporters and they considered ways in which they might secure the backing, or assure the neutrality, of other unions. Gaitskell recorded:

We had a very interesting three hours' discussion, in which Sam talked very freely. . . . It was altogether a very stimulating evening. I have never seen Sam in such good form. He was very anxious obviously that I should start taking the lead in all sorts of ways, and particularly wished that I really was doing something about the finances of the Party. He wanted me to do this, however, not through messing around with the administration of Transport House and the Regions, but through talks with the Unions and speeches in the country. I think his advice is probably sound, and I shall talk to him further.

Desmond appears to have kept out of the exchange, for if he was particularly close to Gaitskell, he was also on good terms with Bevan. The one was the standard bearer of the right wing of the Party, the other of the left, and although Desmond's own sympathies were with the right, he preferred to stay above factional frays and maintain his home as an open forum.

Lord Longford, who had been a close friend of Gaitskell's since their Oxford days when they had shared digs together, met Desmond through Gaitskell. Although 'Hugh was a first-rate economist and had been Chancellor of the Exchequer,' Longford recalls, 'he had no first-hand knowledge of the City and Desmond was invaluable to him.' In his book *Five Lives*, Longford writes about a dinner party at the Hirshfields at which Gaitskell was present. This took place shortly after Gaitskell had made an historic anti-Common Market speech at the 1962 Brighton conference and a few days after Longford had written an article disagreeing with him. The Hirshfields' home again provided a venue where political differences could be aired without old friendships being affected:

> As soon as we met two things were clear. Nothing was going to make Hugh alter his line on the Common Market by an iota. But, short of that, he would do everything within his power to remove any pain that his Brighton speech might have caused. We did not discuss the Common Market for the first two hours. It seemed likely to remain a forbidden subject. . . . We all settled

down to the most carefree of evenings. Somehow or other we got round to the perilous topic. Perhaps Elizabeth [Longford] raised it. She is always far bolder than I am, and in a trice we were all at Hugh hammer and tongs. As soon as one of us stopped, another would take up the tale on behalf of Europe. Desmond and the rest of us deserve some credit perhaps for letting Hugh feel throughout that he was among warm and admiring friends, but it was he who shone. His demeanour, in its patience and forbearance, was almost saint-like, as we all agreed when he left and subsequently.

Given his early years of hardship and the nature of his training, Desmond was careful with money, but when it came to food and wine, he insisted on nothing but the best. An evening meal *chez* Hirshfield might consist of a choice of lamb or beef with a wide variety of vegetables and salads. The desserts usually included crêpes suzettes, Desmond's speciality, which he prepared himself with much spurting of brandy over flickering flames. He once nearly set the flat alight by spilling too much brandy over the crêpes.

The wife of one trade union leader, in writing to thank Bronia for a memorable evening, added: 'We can't hope to return your hospitality in the same style, but will you accept an open invitation to drop in any time you can, or feel like it, to share our bread and dripping.'

Desmond and Bronia had a full and happy life, which left them with little free time. Their favourite form of relaxation was travel. They had one long holiday a year, though given the frequency and extent of their travels, Bronia was not always certain when they were on holiday and when they weren't. They were often in Paris, where Desmond had an office and which they both loved. However, they were at their happiest in Switzerland, usually in Davos, though sometimes in Bad Ragaz, a small watering place near Zürich. In the mornings they walked in the hills. In the afternoons he painted and she read. The paintings, mostly of landscapes and townscapes, with a good eye for detail, gave him great pleasure and show considerable talent, but to Bronia they are minor masterpieces. She is a fairly talented painter herself, mostly of floral subjects in bright colours, but does not allow her work to be mentioned in the same breath as Desmond's.

They also visited America frequently, and once, when crossing the Atlantic on the liner *United States* as part of a British delegation, they found themselves having drinks with the Duke and Duchess of Windsor, after the Duke had asked to meet members of the delegation. Later, the Duchess asked Desmond to dance, and the Duke invited Bronia to join him in a fox-trot. He noticed that she had a foreign accent.

'German?' he asked.

'No, Sir, Polish.'

They conversed in German for a while and he mentioned in passing that the last time he had spoken that language it was to Hermann Goering, at which her voice gave out. But she did ask him and the Duchess for their autographs, which she keeps on the wall of her living-room.

Much as they loved travel, they were always glad to be back in their London flat and, as Desmond readily acknowledged in the letters he sent to Bronia on her birthdays and wedding anniversaries, any success he enjoyed was due to her devotion and the warmth, stability and security she had brought to his life.

They lived in Hanover Gate Mansions for twenty years and during that time entertained almost every well-known figure in the Labour Party from Clement Attlee to Koni Zilliacus, plus guests from many countries where Desmond

The old city of Baden, sketched from the high bridge

had offices. As they entertained frequently, they were frequently entertained, and Bronia has particularly happy memories of a Sunday lunch with the Attlees, who were by then living in retirement in a cottage in Buckinghamshire. They began with an obligatory round of croquet on the lawn, and when they sat down to lunch, the former Prime Minister served the meal.

Though Desmond was close to Attlee – and managed his private financial affairs – he was infinitely closer to Gaitskell, who succeeded him as Party Leader in 1955 and who became an intimate family friend. They normally entertained their guests in the dining-room, but they were familiar enough with Gaitskell and his wife Dora to entertain them in the kitchen. The Gaitskells treated them with the same easy informality at their home in Frognal Gardens, north London.

'They were part of our family,' says Bronia, 'and we were part of theirs. With others we discussed politics or the events of the day, with the Gaitskells we could discuss personal problems.' She recalls one particular evening when they all helped themselves out of a large cast-iron pot in the middle of the kitchen table.

She had a particular affinity with Dora – later Baroness Gaitskell – who, like her, stemmed from an Orthodox Jewish family, and could relax in her company in a way that she could not relax with anyone else. With the Attlees she was a guest; with the Gaitskells she felt at home.

Gaitskell was an academic, which Desmond was not, but he came to admire Desmond's clear mind, his analytic powers and administrative skills. Shortly after he became Leader, he invited Desmond to reorganise the finances of the Party and put its whole administration on a businesslike basis. Old Labour hands were startled by his intervention and did not quite know what to make of him, but he was brisk and efficient and, within a few months, had transformed the machinery of the Party. At Gaitskell's request he also brought together a panel of industrialists and businessmen with Labour sympathies who could advise the Party on economic policy.

Gaitskell felt that Labour sometimes paid too much attention to theory and too little to the practicalities of economic life, and Desmond, so to speak, became his contact with the market. Desmond may never have believed in socialism, but he did believe in Gaitskellism, which he found humane, pragmatic, far-seeing, open-minded and untrammelled by doctrine or dogma. When Gaitskell died in January 1963 at the age of fifty-six, both he and Bronia were shattered. They felt as if they had lost a member of their own family.

'Desmond was in tears,' Bronia recalls. 'He couldn't speak, he was shaking. I was in tears myself. We knew he was very ill, but we liked to think he would pull through.' Apart from the personal sense of loss, Desmond saw in the death of Gaitskell the death of both a mentor and guide and of the sort of socialism he could cheerfully work with and work for.

At the time of his death, Gaitskell's popularity was greater than that of Prime Minister Harold Macmillan and a Labour Party victory was being predicted at the next general election. Had Gaitskell become Prime Minister, Desmond's star would have risen with him; as it was, at the age of fifty he more or less had to start again.

Harold Wilson, who was elected the next Leader of the Labour Party and who became Prime Minister in 1964, had always viewed Gaitskell and his followers with suspicion, believing them to be enemies of the left. However, he had a high regard for Jewish talent in general, and for Desmond's ability in particular. He was familiar with his work for the trade union movement, especially the formation of the Trades Union Unit Trust in 1961, and the Foundation on Automation and Employment, which Desmond set up the following year, fitted in well with Wilson's own plans to launch a 'white-hot technological revolution'. As Lord Longford has noted, Desmond was soon to win Wilson's complete confidence.

Wilson was also familiar with Desmond's work for Gaitskell and, when he lost the election in 1970, invited him to reorganise his private office. It was a major undertaking and Desmond prepared a radical plan, which satisfied Wilson but which proved a little too radical for the old pros at head office. They feared a diminution in their authority and resented the intrusion of someone whom they regarded as an outsider upon their private preserve. Much to Desmond's chagrin, the scheme was quietly dropped.

Desmond also belonged to the Labour Finance and Industry Group, which kept Labour in touch with the thinking of the market and which also helped to finance the Party's election campaigns. Wilson used to phone him up for an informal chat on a variety of problems.

By 1967 Desmond had been an active member of the Labour movement for twenty-five years. He had performed innumerable services both for the Party and the trade unions, some paid but many unpaid. Now that Labour was back in office he had reason to expect that his efforts would enjoy recognition; in his English way, he believed that all good things come to those who wait.

Bronia was on holiday with her mother-in-law Lily in Deauville when Desmond arrived unexpectedly with a broad grin on his face, threw his arms round her and addressed her as Lady Hirshfield.

'Lady who?' asked Lily.

'I've just been made a Lord,' Desmond explained.

'Oh my goodness,' Lily screamed, 'what does that make me?'

'The Queen Mother,' said Desmond, and the three of them grasped hands and did a little dance on the sandy shore.

Bronia was of course overjoyed, because it confirmed her belief that fate had destined him for a peerage. Although ambitious for him, she was not ambitious for herself. She had always thought of herself as a lady and, since her marriage to Desmond, had conducted herself as a woman of rank. The title confirmed not only his status but hers.

His phones, both at home and in his office, did not stop ringing. Letters poured in from all directions and Lord Longford was among the first to congratulate him:

My Dear Desmond,

I am writing to tell you how delighted I am to learn from the Prime Minister that you are about to join us in the Lords. You will be a great accession of strength and warmly welcomed by everyone, particularly by myself. I know that Eddie Shackleton, the Deputy Leader, Frank Beswick and the other Whips, and I, will always do everything to be of assistance.

Lord Sainsbury was equally enthusiastic:

I cannot tell you how delighted I am, though not surprised, that you are joining our ranks at the House of Lords. Needless to say, with your great experience, you will be able to make a valuable contribution to our debates and I look forward to seeing you frequently when we reassemble in the autumn.

Desmond's coat of arms contained several Jewish motifs, including the candelabra as a symbol of light, which was also the symbol of the state of Israel. He took his motto from Isaiah 1:18: 'Come now and let us reason together', which summed up his, possibly naïve, conviction that given a readiness to talk, a modicum of goodwill and more than a modicum of patience, no problem was insoluble. He assumed the title of Lord Hirshfield of Holborn.

His sponsors were Lord Robens, the former Chairman of the National Coal Board, and Lord Carron, the former head of the engineering union, both of whom had worked with him in various capacities, and who were his principal lieutenants in the formation of the Foundation for Automation and Employment.

He was fifty-four, which was not old for a lord, nor for the sort of ambitions which Bronia still had for him She felt that he had hitherto shone in obscurity and believed that the Lords would enable him to shine in public and would add thrust to his upward flight. The best, she was confident, was still ahead and, though he was to suffer more than one setback, he was about to enter upon the most exciting phase of his career.

7

A Man of Vision

Desmond was awarded his peerage largely on the strength of two innovations, the Trades Union Unit Trust (TUUT) and the Foundation on Automation and Employment. The first is still flourishing, the second is no more, but for the best of reasons. The ideas he put forward have become part of the national agenda, even if he could not always carry the trade unions with him.

He found in working with the trade union movement that the most radical of unionists were often the most conservative of men, and that Low's famous caricature of the TUC as a shaggy old lumbering cart-horse, if anything, flattered the movement. He discovered early in his career that they were reluctant to introduce machinery even into their book-keeping procedures, so that accounts, in many cases, were still written by hand in huge dusty ledgers by a small army of clerks long after most business concerns had gone over to machines.

More seriously, many unions still entrusted their internal audits to laymen so that in the National Union of Railwaymen, for example, which in 1956 had an income of nearly £1,500,000, the internal audit was carried out by two engine-drivers and a time-keeper. They were honest, hardworking and conscientious men, said Desmond, but were about as capable of auditing books as he was of driving an engine. The defects of the system came to light only when a cashier committed suicide after embezzling more than £10,000.

There had been few strikes during the war, and though there were a great many in the immediate post-war decades they were mostly unofficial and did not call for the use of strike funds. Moreover, the union movement as a whole had grown from some six million members in 1938 to nearly eight million at the end of the war. As a result, it had built up massive reserves of capital, which were invested in gilt-edged securities. Desmond showed that given the rate of inflation, the investments had lost about £20 million in value in the immediate post-war years, whereas, if properly handled, they could have appreciated by the same amount. In 1960 he therefore proposed the creation of a trades union unit trust, through which the unions would invest in a wide range of equities.

The idea seemed simple enough and foolproof, but it aroused considerable opposition. Some denounced sell-out to capitalism, which would help to prop up a system the unions had sworn to destroy. Others argued that workers with a stake in an industry would be inhibited in wage negotiations. Others were unhappy with the idea of speculative investment, no matter how slight the risk, and argued that as unions had always invested in gilts in the past, they could see no reason why they shouldn't continue to do so in the future.

One reason why they shouldn't, said Desmond, was that gilts were yielding about 3 per cent while the rate of inflation was nearer 5 per cent. 'Equity investing,' he argued, 'will enable unions to share in the industrial productivity their members have helped to build.' It would also, he believed, give unions a closer sense of involvement in the prosperity of the economy as a whole and would, in the long run, improve the climate of industrial relations.

Also, he added, there was 'an educational purpose to be served by investment in British industry. It would give trade union leaders and their membership greater insight into the function of capital. It would show the need for risk capital in industry and what dividends are all about.'

He invited small groups of union leaders around for a drink at Hanover Gate Mansions to discuss his idea in detail and talks continued late into the night, with Bronia padding around in an elegant house-coat and embroidered slippers serving sandwiches and beer.

Desmond was particularly anxious to bring his friend Frank Cousins round to his ideas. Cousins, a former lorry driver, was head of the Transport and General Workers' Union, which, with more than one and a half million members, was the biggest union in the country. Desmond believed that with the TGWU in the bag, most of the other unions would immediately follow, but Cousins, an inveterate socialist and flag-bearer of the Labour left, would have no part it. As a result, the process became rather more laborious. Desmond was nevertheless able to win over the railwaymen, the electricians, the Durham miners and a number of other major unions, with assets running into many millions.

He finally launched the TUUT in July 1961, with himself as Chairman, under the management of Hill Samuel and a board of eight directors, two from Hill Samuel, one from the Orion Bank, one from Rothschilds, one from the Bank of England, and three from the Labour movement (the first three being Douglas Jay, Sid Greene of the National Union of Railwaymen and Alf Allen of the Shop Distributive and Allied Workers).

It got off to a slow start but soon snowballed. By 1971 some sixty unions had joined the scheme and within those ten years the TUUT had made a profit of 135 per cent, outstripping even the performance of the Stock Market as a whole. In 1975 it came top of *The Times* Unit Trust League.

It was not, however, all plain-sailing because some of the unions wanted assurances that their money was not going to companies with interests in South Africa, or other politically sensitive areas, or to companies with a poor record of industrial relations. To cope with such fears Desmond set up a unit holders' investment committee of fifteen trade unionists with the power to ban investments in companies, or even whole industries, where they fell short of certain specified standards, but it has never had cause to exercise its veto.

In 1983 Desmond retired from the Trust, his judgement abundantly vindicated.

At first only unions could invest in the TUUT. Later, individual unionists were also admitted, and to encourage their participation the minimum investment was reduced to £20, while management charges were reduced to 2 per cent instead of the usual 4 per cent.

The TUUT – since renamed the TU British Trust – continues to flourish even while the trade union movement as a whole is in decline. Between 1985 and 1995 the value of its assets increased by some 225 per cent and now stands at over £85 million. While its investments are confined to blue-chip enterprises, all sections of the economy are represented in its portfolio: building, engineering, petrochemicals, banks and insurance, retailing, mining and property. Desmond lived long enough to draw satisfaction from the fact that the Trust also did particularly well out of British Telecom, British Gas, British Airways and other privatised industries. The very idea of such investments would have involved him in a battle royal in the early days of the Trust. They did not occasion a whimper in the later ones.

By 1960 Desmond had been working with trade unions for some twenty years, and though liked and admired as an able accountant and a decent bloke, with an attractive wife who gave good parties, he was not regarded as one of the lads. No one would have dreamt of calling him Brother Desmond, let alone Comrade. His advice might be sought on some tax problem, but never on matters of policy, and he never presumed to give it. His campaign for the TUUT, therefore, represented something of a departure and it must be said that the suspicion of some unionists that he was trying to drag the movement into the capitalist domain was well-founded. But then he had always believed – though he had never spelt it out in so many words – that what was good for capital was good for both labour and the country, and that high wages and good working conditions were, in the long term, dependent on profits.

His tactics were essentially Fabian, and instead of making a frontal assault on the left-wing principles of the movement – for which he was in any case ill-equipped – he introduced his ideas subtly and unobtrusively in the guise of plain common sense, which was, indeed, how he saw them. The TUUT was one example; the Foundation on Automation and Employment was another.

In 1957, through the good offices of his friend Joe Godson, the Labour attaché at the American Embassy, Desmond spent two months in the United States studying the American taxation system and productivity in American industry. He went armed with introductions from Hugh Gaitskell and other public figures and was received by senior government officials and major industrialists and bankers. He was deeply impressed by the pace of technological change. He saw the first computer in the world in operation at Stanford University, a vast machine occupying an entire building, and immediately sensed the implications of the device. Unlike most members of the Labour Party, he became a great admirer of America and American briskness, dynamism, the readiness to take risks and the ability to face up to the challenges of the future.

Early in 1962 US Industries (USI), a vast company involved in the manufacture and distribution of automotive machinery, and the International Association of Machinists, one of the largest unions in America, launched the American Foundation on Automation and Employment with John Snyder, head of the one, and A. I. Hayes, head of the other, as co-Chairmen. Theodore Kheel, a distinguished labour lawyer, became Secretary and Treasurer. The organisation was financed by USI, which also had extensive interests in the United Kingdom. USI, of course, benefited hugely and directly from the spread of automation, but Snyder was a far-seeing tycoon who recognised the social costs involved and was anxious to ameliorate them as far as possible. However, the moving spirit behind the Foundation was Kheel. Theodore and Anne Kheel had met Desmond and Bronia in 1962 at the home of their mutual friends, Herman and Helene Cooper, in New York. Herman was a tough labour lawyer and Helene was a great hostess, whose parties were attended by New York's social elite. Kheel and Desmond became, and remained, close friends. Kheel came to regard Hanover Gate Mansions as his home from home during his many visits to London. Kheel, like Desmond, believed that the 'us' and 'them' attitudes between capital and labour were inimical to both, and that industrial and economic progress depended on co-operation and not confrontation. The Foundation thus symbolised everything that they had striven for.

'George Meany, then head of the American labor movement, had called automation a curse,' Kheel recalled, 'but the general belief was that it could not and should not be stopped and that the impact on employment could best be addressed by solving the job losses that automation was creating. The labor and industry members of our Foundation strongly believed that it would be very helpful if a companion foundation to work with us was created in England. We held this view in the light of our common heritage and comparable institutions.'

He found a natural ally in Desmond, who, with his customary energy, quickly set up a parallel Foundation in Britain with William Carron, President of the Amalgamated Engineering Union, whose members were most immediately affected by the spread of automation, as Chairman, and Lord Robens, Chairman of the National Coal Board, as Vice-Chairman. Desmond functioned as Secretary and Treasurer. He presumably could not find a British backer and, in an agreement signed on 21 November 1962, USI Inc. undertook to pay the Foundation a minimum of £10,000 a year for five years, 'by means of a levy on the sale or lease of automation machines within the United Kingdom'.

In December the American Foundation sponsored an International Research Conference on the impact of automation, at the London School of Economics, which was attended by leading educators and scholars from America and more than a dozen universities in Britain and western Europe. The British Foundation had only a walk-on part in its deliberations, but after the conference the two organisations held a series of meetings to debate strategies and co-ordinate activities.

As Kheel has written, the two Foundations worked in close harmony with each other, helping to 'create public awareness of the seriousness of the problem'. Kheel introduced Desmond to many leading American figures in the worlds of politics, labour and business, who 'were invariably impressed with his familiarity with events in this country and his ability to enlighten them with relevant information from overseas'. As Kheel fondly recalls:

> Desmond was a proper gentleman. He knew and honored all social and diplomatic rules and requisite amenities. I remember being told by Desmond when, as a brash American abroad, I sometimes overlooked a rule of suitable British conduct, that 'You can't do that here.' But I saw another side of Desmond particularly when he visited America. Desmond was completely at home in whatever place he was in. He was also up to the minute on what was happening in politics, society and business in all locations.

The impact of automation on employment had been debated at a trade union conference in Margate as early as 1955. The Department of Scientific and Industrial Research produced a wide-ranging study in 1956, followed a year later by Pollocks' 'The Economic and Social Consequences of Automation', which became required reading both for trade unions and industry, and which might have served as the text for Desmond's Foundation. By 1962, moreover, large parts of the petrochemical industry – including the vast new Esso refinery at Fawley – were largely automated. Desmond nevertheless felt that the matter was not being approached with sufficient urgency, especially by trade unionists, if only because they had not been able to make up their minds whether it was a good thing or a bad one.

Desmond thought that, on balance, it was a good thing, but, whether good or bad, it was inevitable. He also felt that the social and economic problems which would ensue called for immediate action. The future, he kept stressing, was already here. 'Britain,' he said, 'needs more and more technology more and more quickly in order to compete with overseas producers. If we are unable to compete we shall lose out, which will cause far greater unemployment than if we foster rapid technology.'

However, he was primarily concerned with the human dimension: 'We must make sure that people do not become just cogs in the wheel and get thrown out of work. In future instead of having one career in a lifetime we will have two or three. We must attune people from childhood in the notion of relocation.' He anticipated much longer holidays, a shorter working week and even shorter working lives, and warned that this too could bring its problems. People, he said, 'should know how to use their leisure time sensibly and not in depravities'. As a result, he launched a scheme in co-operation with the Schools Council to provide an information service on technology and leisure to children in their late teens. Such ideas may seem commonplace now, but they were fairly visionary in 1962.

The initial impact of technological change was on manufacturing industry, but Desmond envisaged that white-collar jobs would also soon be affected on a massive scale. On the other hand new opportunities would be created. Schools would have to take account of the change, while a large part of the existing labour force would have to adapt to the new opportunities.

He was not particularly cheered by what he saw ahead, for he admired the traditional skills of many of the old craft unions which he was proud to number among his clients. One could not prevent change, but the Foundation on Automation and Employment was designed to mitigate its effects.

The Foundation, however, though concerned with a major issue, was never a major undertaking with its own premises, machinery and full-time staff. It operated on a shoestring and was managed by Desmond himself with the help of his tireless secretary Betty Arkell, from his offices in Norwich House. To all intents and purposes Desmond was the British Foundation on Automation and Employment.

He was also a member of the Council, which was composed of prominent industrialists, trade unionists and academics, including Norman Chester, Warden of Nuffield College, Oxford; Lord Nelson, head of English Electric; and Sir Leon Bagrit, whose company, Elliott-Automation, was a pioneer in this field and was the first in Europe to be devoted to automation. In 1964 Bagrit was invited to give the Reith Lectures on the BBC and chose automation as his subject. The vast audience he attracted greatly facilitated Desmond's effort to push the matter to the forefront of national debate.

Lord Robens, a robust, hearty figure, was a former miners' leader who became head of the National Coal Board and a leading industrialist. He could therefore bring the perspectives of both sides of industry to the challenge of automation. Desmond admired his alacrity, judgement and managerial skills, and thus, perhaps inevitably, he assumed a crucial role in the Foundation.

The Foundation sponsored lectures, conferences, seminars and research, and produced a spate of publications. Its primary objectives were to ease the introduction of automation and other methods of production and productivity; to educate and train employees to understand and operate automation; to avoid the unfavourable effects on employees of the introduction of automation; and to aid in transitional arrangements, relocation and retraining. As Kheel says, all these aims pointed to one logical solution: the creation of new jobs through expanded economic growth.

In 1965 the Foundation organised a three-day conference at the National Staff College in Chalfont St Giles, which was attended by eminent industrialists, bankers, senior civil servants, academics and lawyers. The star turn, however, was Frank Cousins, who a year earlier had been appointed by Harold Wilson to the newly created post of Minister of Technology to give practical expression to Wilson's vision of the 'white-hot technological revolution', which he had pronounced at the Scarborough Labour Conference in 1963.

Desmond may not have been able to win Cousins over to the benefits of the TUUT, but they shared much the same views on automation and employment, as Cousins made clear both at Chalfont St Giles and at a Labour conference in January 1966. His speech, in good part, read like one of the pamphlets produced by the Foundation on Automation and employment:

> This is one of the most vital issues of the labour movement. There is no more important task for the Labour Party than to ensure that we secure the benefits of automation without bringing with it the misery and upheavals caused to so many by the first industrial revolution.
>
> I don't believe that we need fear automation, but it is my duty and the task of all of us to show those we represent that if we deal with this in a proper way, they too have no need to fear.

To avoid dislocation and unemployment, he called for a massive retraining scheme much on the lines advocated by Desmond: 'It may not always be easy for a man to change his job in response to changing circumstances,' he said, 'but

I am sure that the trade union view is not that a man should have the same job for ever.'

Unfortunately, a few months later Cousins fell out with Wilson over the Government's wages policy and walked out of his job. Once he was back at the helm of the TGWU, he was a good deal less positive about automation than he had been as a Minister. It represented a considerable set-back to Desmond.

In September 1965 Desmond was invited to address a large gathering of industrialists and lawyers in New York on the challenge of automation in Britain. 'Automation,' he began, 'is a continuous advance into uncertainty, and chance favours the prepared mind.' Britain, he had to admit, was not all that prepared. 'In the United States you have been living with automation as a daily fact of life for at least the past fifteen years. In my country we are only now coming to grips with the challenge. We often appear to be psychologically caged by the past. It is sometimes as if our heritage of power, influence and world status – now diminished but by no means extinct – compels a mocking picture of those nations who now challenge us by appearing more ready to innovate and adapt themselves to new ideas and different values. It frequently seems to me that we British are perhaps anxious to protect ourselves from change by an over-emphasis on past achievement.'

Having said this, he pointed to major British industries which had escaped the thraldom of the past, but he was perhaps unfortunate in alighting on the coal industry to illustrate his claim that one can introduce major technological change without social interest or industrial disruption. Desmond's association with the miners and mining industry went back to his earliest days as an accountant, and his sentimental feelings about both tended to cloud his judgement. In common with much of the country, the picture of the helmeted miner, hardy, resilient, cheerful, his smiling features encrusted in coal-dust, embodied his vision of the working man, and like most of his colleagues in the Labour movement, he failed to see the bleak prospects which the coal industry actually faced.

He was on happier ground when he turned to the Esso oil refinery at Fawley as 'one of the most remarkable success stories in British labour relations in recent years', for it had abandoned 'such practices as excessive overtime, the use of craftsmen's mates and resistance to job switching', and had amply compensated employees for doing so. 'The Fawley example', he continued, 'was being followed by other companies', and he was confident that British industry would be able to tread 'through the automation minefield without touching off a violent social explosion'.

His speech was, on the whole, a masterly analysis of the British economy in the mid-1960s, succinct, wide-ranging and well-informed, but – as his references to mining suggested – not wholly free of wishful thinking.

In 1967 he devoted part of his maiden speech in the House of Lords to the work of the Foundation on Automation and Employment. 'Management', he said, 'bears the responsibility for taking decisions to introduce automation or data processing and must recognise the need for boldness and for educating middle-management to be receptive to change. Responsible trade union leadership knows – and the TUC itself has said – that more automation is needed urgently in Britain, because without it there would most likely be greater unemployment due to greater foreign productivity and competition.'

The subject was in some respects timely, for he was speaking in an atmosphere of crisis induced by the devaluation of sterling. The situation, he felt, called for a national consensus: 'This is an hour in the economic history of Britain when Party political infighting ought to be temporarily halted; when harmful debate over devaluation should be cast aside and searching after scapegoats called off – while everybody in this Realm unites to win the battle for exports, to speed the advance towards greater productivity and to stride rapidly forward through this great new age of technology.' He tried to avoid any partisan tone both in this speech and later, and he liked to think that his approach to the problems of automation could win the support of all sections of the public.

It was not, as he was himself aware, the sort of issue which provoked headlines, and his work for the Foundation did not excite much attention, but his expertise on the matter was widely recognised. When, for example, Harold Wilson went to America in 1970 to address a conference on automation, he turned to Desmond for advice on the points he should raise.

Desmond took the human dimension more seriously than the economic one, as he explained in an interview with the *Investors Chronicle* in October 1974:

> There was a a notion that automation would cause unemployment, but we realised that the unions would solve the problem by negotiating shorter hours. The problem is not so much unemployment as how to deal with increased leisure, people have to be educated to know how best to use their leisure hours, in cultural pursuits for example.

This was an issue to which he would return at every opportunity and which had by then already shaped his own future.

In 1967 the British Foundation, together with its US counterpart and the Swedish Employers' Federation, the Swedish Trade Union Confederation and the Swedish

Central Organisation of Salaried Employees, organised an international conference on automation, full employment and a balanced economy. Rome was chosen as the venue for no better reason than it happened to be an attractive place to meet. No Italian organisation was involved, though it was graced by the presence of the Minister of Labour and the Minister of Science, both of whom gave eloquent speeches. Prime Minister Harold Wilson sent a message, which possibly summed up the theme of the conference: 'The Industrial Revolution 150 years ago was carried out without regard to human beings. Our task in this age is to temper the technological revolution with humanity.' The same point was made more succinctly by the Italian Minister of Science, who said: 'Man should assert himself to be the master and not the victim of technological change.'

The dilemma which faced participants, however, was implicit in the title of the conference. One could have automation and full employment, and one could have automation and a balanced economy, but it was rather more difficult to assure all three, and most of the speakers tried to suggest ways in which this could be done.

A further international conference was held two years later in Jerusalem, which was Desmond's particular baby, for he was a great admirer of the Histadruth, the Confederation of Labour, Israel's TUC, which was one of the sponsors of the conference. As we have seen, Desmond had encouraged the unions to acquire a stake in British industry. The Histadruth had more than a stake in Israeli industry. It owned Koor Industries, which was one of the largest conglomerates in the country, as well as a large bank (with which Desmond was associated), a major insurance company, a publishing house and a daily paper. To Desmond, it was everything a trade union movement should be, and he never missed an opportunity to quote it as an example.

The Rome conference had been a great success; the Jerusalem conference was even greater, for apart from the issues raised at the conference itself, there were workshops which discussed them in detail, and the gathering excited wide attention in the Israeli press. Desmond was particularly gratified by the event.

Sadly some twenty years later Koor Industries all but succumbed to the sort of problems raised by the conference, for while it encouraged automation, it continued to keep employees on the payroll and might have collapsed but for the intervention of the Government.

The amount of work when there was a conference in prospect was colossal, but, as Mrs Arkell recalls, Desmond thrived on it. 'He was a workaholic and the more he had to do the happier he was.' While Desmond attended all the conferences and presided at some of the sessions, he was rarely one of the speakers. If he enjoyed the trappings of fame, he did not particularly care for prominence and preferred the role of *éminence grise*. Moreover, he felt slightly overawed by the company of scholars.

The Foundation, which later changed its name to the Foundation on Automation and Human Development, may have made an invaluable contribution to academic debate, but it had only a limited impact on the people he was most anxious to influence – the trade unions and trade unionists. This was especially true of the printers, who, ironically enough, were his own clients. They were highly paid and highly qualified craftsmen and were understandably afraid that their skills would be made redundant by technological change. Yet, instead of trying to adapt to it, they did their damnedest to check it and were eventually destroyed by it.

Desmond understood the anxieties of craftsmen trying to preserve a market for their craft and drew no comfort from the fact that his worst prognostications were confirmed by events. However, not all the unions were Luddites. The electricians – who had by then amalgamated with the Plumbers' Union – were also among his clients, and were at one time the most recalcitrant and bloody-minded of all the unions. After an internal revolution, they became one of the most enlightened and adaptable and eventually took over many of the jobs previously handled by the printers.

Desmond's heraldic motto, 'Come now and let us reason together', hadn't worked. Mrs Thatcher's motto, 'Come let us bludgeon the unions', proved rather more effective. If Desmond had any thoughts on the matter, he never voiced them.

As we have seen, he was careful not only to stress the challenge posed by automation but the social trans-formation it would bring and the opportunities it would offer. Decline in some areas, he argued, would be redressed by growth in others, especially in travel and tourism. He was convinced that, with the spread of automation, people would have longer holidays and a shorter working week (where they were employed at all) and that the leisure industry would grow faster than any other, both in de-veloping and developed countries. He therefore began to concentrate more and more on the needs of the hotel and catering trade and became one of the leading authorities in the field, consulted by governments and public companies on their development projects. This led, as we shall see, to the formation of Horwath & Horwath (UK).

The Foundation was finally wound up in 1986 and Desmond used its residuary funds to endow two prizes for post-graduate students in Industrial Relations at the London School of Economics.

8

In the Lords

Desmond made his maiden speech in the House of Lords on 21 November 1967, and Bronia was there to see him and hear him. She had come not merely to listen to a speech but to witness an apotheosis. She had, of course, seen him take his seat, but that was merely a spasm of pageantry which was over almost before she could take it in. Here he was finally in action, Lord Hirshfield of Holborn, addressing the elite of the land, and she gloried in every minute of it.

His topic was the devaluation of sterling, which had just taken place. There was talk of national bankruptcy and the whole debate was held in an atmosphere of crisis. He, however, characteristically opened on a light-hearted note: 'My Lords, earlier today it was suggested to me that I should acquaint your Lordships of the fact that I am an accountant. I suppose that was in case it was thought that, on a day like this, on seeing me stand up for the first time your Lordships might think that I was the bailiff. A little later, by coincidence, it happened that I was lunching with the President of my professional institute and with members of his council. I asked him what he thought about the way I should introduce myself. He said: "Of course you must not mention you are an accountant; it is unethical." Therefore I have not done so.'

He said that he was given to understand that maiden speeches should be non-controversial and brief. 'In that respect,' he said, 'taking account of earlier speeches this afternoon, I found the average time taken was 21.43 minutes. I will try to devalue that down to 14.3 minutes . . .'. He in fact spoke for twenty minutes and dealt with the fairly hackneyed subject of the relations between management and labour. He could, however, speak with unique authority for he had experience of both, and had used the opportunity to bring together, as he put it, 'the heads of business and the unions to talk with one another in a relaxed mood and in utter openness, instead of their merely meeting together over the trials and stresses of the bargaining table'. As an example of such co-operation, he mentioned the Trades Union Unit Trust and the Foundation on Automation and Employment.

He blamed the previous Tory administration for some of the difficulties the country now faced, but added that mistakes had also been made by Labour: '. . . too much was attempted at once in the sphere of taxation. I consider that the corporation tax and the capital gains tax, both very desirable, would have been best introduced with, say, a gap of a year between them. I am sure too that the selective employment tax hardly succeeded in its declared intention,' and he called for an urgent review of the entire taxation system.

He quoted with approval the words of Lord Cooper, a trade union peer, that there was 'a need for modernisation of the trade union movement. We have to recognise the priority of the national interest over our sectional interest, and that in industrial bargaining the strike should be the weapon of last resort.' He endorsed every point Cooper had made and closed with a call for greater 'industrial discipline on the part both of management and labour'. However, he did not suggest how this might be achieved.

As a successful accountant and businessman who had served on several public boards and was involved in numerous charities, he was often invited to make after-dinner speeches and, having a flair for showmanship, he was usually happy to comply. The House of Lords was rather different. It was, as he himself observed, full of men who were at the top of their professions and who could speak with authority and insight on a great variety of topics. They were not predisposed to laugh at his jokes or applaud his perorations, especially as – like most members – he sometimes found himself addressing a near-empty House.

Yet even as a maiden speaker in a fairly full House, he was not for a moment overawed by either his distinguished audience or his majestic surroundings. He did not have anything particularly original to say, but spoke with fluency and confidence on several topics, all of them closely linked, and expressed himself in clear, down-to-earth terms. It was a good start, and when he finished Bronia was half tempted to rush downstairs and throw her arms around him.

The eminent economist Lord Robbins, who followed, described his observations as 'thought-provoking and temperate', and he was complimented by Lord Jellicoe, a Tory peer, on 'a quiet, lucid and independent-minded maiden speech'. Lord Soskice, who had served as Solicitor-General and Home Secretary under Attlee, was more enthusiastic: 'What a splendid speech! Penetrating, balanced, dignified and perfectly phrased and delivered. It obviously made a very big impression on the House and was a great personal triumph. You clearly have a great future here.'

For a maiden speech it was good, and Desmond seems to have taken the general reaction at its face value. He sent copies of his speech to all his friends, which engendered further praise. Perhaps emboldened by this, he went on to make ten speeches – none of them short – in the course of the next eight months, which would not have been a lot for a full-time politician, but was a lot for a full-time accountant with a large and demanding clientele.

Moreover, he was not given to impromptu interjections. Every speech was the result of careful preparation, research and lengthy cogitation. Mrs Arkell recalls typing draft after draft, and Bronia has vivid memories of him at his desk in the late hours of the night, while she came and went with jugs of coffee. (She could not think of sleep while he was awake.)

He was an effective speaker, but speeches were something of an ordeal for him. Possibly because they were an ordeal, they represented a challenge which he was determined to surmount and which, to an extent, he did surmount. As his speeches were to show, he was also a man with a mission.

On 14 February 1968, in a debate on the Government fuel policy, he denounced the reluctance of the private sector to invest in areas where successive pit closures had given rise to high unemployment. He then recommended the example of Israel, where the first factories in development areas were planned, financed, built and managed by the joint action of the Government and the trade union movement: 'Now with plants constructed and operating in several places, and with housing and labour adequately organised, private enterprise is following the lead. There are even instances where private enterprise has since acquired interests in Government and trade union sponsored industrial plants.' He could speak with particular authority on the subject for he was a member of the London board of the Bank Hapoalim, one of Israel's largest banks, which was owned by the Histadruth.

He often had cause to speak about co-operation, or the lack of it, between the two sides of industry. In Israel the trade unions themselves to a large extent represented both sides, and he was to evoke the example of Israel again in subsequent debates.

A week later he spoke on youth and education and adapted a famous line from President Kennedy to suggest that, 'in looking for new ways of helping young people, we should ask not what more we can do for them but what they can do in their own way for others.' He urged the Government to allow 'youth to share the responsibility of accelerated change, to shape the new world in which they must live, and above all to have total responsibility, and not just tutelage, for areas that are given to them to explore'.

This, perhaps inevitably, brought him to the Foundation on Automation and Employment, and he made the point that old educational patterns would have to be revised to keep pace with technological change because many traditional skills would be rendered obsolete, and one's working life in future could involve several periods of re-training. Action was needed now, he said, and announced that the FAE would be supplying a selected number of schools and colleges with rudimentary computers to prepare them for the changes ahead. He closed with a Chinese proverb:

'When planning for a year – sow corn.
When planning for a decade – plant trees.
When planning for life – train and educate men.'

Twenty years later there were computers even in primary schools, but in 1968 the whole idea may have seemed a trifle fanciful.

On 29 February he was on his feet again, this time on the Commonwealth Immigrants Bill. The issue had been raised as a matter of urgency because the expulsion of East African Asians – most of them holders of British passports – from Uganda threatened a major influx of new immigrants and the Labour Government was rushing a Bill through Parliament to restrict their entry. Desmond, possibly remembering the difficulties which Jewish refugees had encountered in the 1930s, and the interventions he had made on their behalf, opposed it with vehemence in what was perhaps the most telling intervention of his career.

He felt bound to speak out, he explained, because he himself had benefited from Britain's traditions of hospitality, and as proof he held up the British passport acquired by his immigrant grandfather as well as his Austrian work permit, both dog-eared and stained, but both symbolic. 'I am thankful to the Almighty', he said, 'that my grandfather could come to this fair land, and eternally grateful, as he was, that he could sojourn here in peace and replant his roots. I mention these personal things for they are a small piece of Britain's greatness, and bear witness to its humanity to thousands who might otherwise have suffered or perished.' The Bill, he said, 'enhances the notion of racial discrimination by introducing a selective control on one section of coloured immigrants and it creates suffering and distrust'. He agreed that some restrictions were necessary, but felt that they should be more equitably and humanely applied.

At the same time, he called for greater efforts to 'integrate the coloured community which already exists in Britain. In housing, schooling and, indeed, the whole range of services, there is an urgent need for more vigorous integrationist policies, supported by adequate finance.' He referred to instances of racial discrimination in housing, employment and in various consumer services, and while he was aware that legislation could not banish discrimination entirely, it was 'a necessary foundation for building racial harmony'.

His speeches on other issues were of a cerebral nature and derived from his experience as a businessman and an accountant, but when he touched on racialism he spoke from the heart. He returned to the subject a few months later in a debate on the Race Relations Bill.

He regarded racialism as one of the major ills of western society and was surprised that the measure should have encountered serious opposition from the Tory benches. He himself believed that the legislation to curb racialism, if anything, did not go far enough.

The Jew, he said, 'has been the victim down the ages of propaganda of the pattern which – alas! – is now heard here, and which has been affecting the most fair-minded citizens. So it is a time for the Jew to stand up fearlessly and give an example of humanity towards other minority groups. . . . There is one more reason why the Jew cannot sit back and allow racialism to grow. If he is true to his religion and upbringing he recognises that man was created in the image of God – not white, not black, but man, every man.' He closed with a quotation from an eminent American rabbi, Abraham Heschel: 'God is every man's pedigree. He is either the father of all men or no man. The image of God is either in every man or in no man.'

On 19 June 1968 he spoke on the students' revolt which helped to topple the French Government and which provoked turmoil on university campuses all over Europe and America. He admitted that his own particular qualifications to speak on students and education were limited: 'I am told I went to fourteen schools. I can remember eight of them. And I remember at one of those eight I was poisoned and first came to this great City with typhus as a result of that poisoning.' Another school he ran away from, he added amid laughter, 'was called Wilson's Grammar School', but he had nevertheless contrived to get something of an education.

He said that though he had campaigned fervently for the welfare state, it had its drawbacks and left many people with the feeling that their lives were 'to a dangerous extent subject to the management and will of others. The structures we have developed for our social services, like the administrative structures which characterise industry, allow no place for the individual to participate in the decision-making processes.' Many people have their reservations about the welfare state today, but for a Labour peer to give voice to them in 1968 verged on the revolutionary and displayed his independence of mind in an emphatic way.

Turning to the universities in particular, he argued that their problems arose partly from rapid expansion and the growth of the permissive society as well as from the impatience of students to grab their share of affluence. However, he felt that the problems were being exploited by a 'militant minority which was trying to destroy existing institutions, but has no positive proposals to offer'.

He combined sympathy for the young with the feeling that students should be made to understand their own limitations. 'British universities', he said, 'are moving rapidly towards integrating students more efficiently into decision-making committees, but there are limits to the process. Young people who are learners do not have either the experience or accumulated knowledge or wisdom to decide on major questions of university policies.'

Desmond soon established himself as a fairly regular

speaker because he had strong feelings on a wide variety of issues and felt duty-bound to express them. On the whole, his speeches were well received. But then came an incident which became engraved on his subconscious as the Carrington Affair.

In June 1968 the sixth Lord Carrington, whose title dated back to 1796, and who was to become a leading member of Mrs Thatcher's administration, interrupted a speech that Desmond was making. He also complained that 'some life peers spoke too often and for too long and on subjects outside their experience.' Desmond felt that the remark was not only uncalled for, but was specifically directed at him, and he did not take long to reply: '. . . some peers of the other rank or kind, who seldom appear in your Lordships' House, tend to crowd in at the wrong times and vote without sufficient self-discipline and thought. But if in the minds of the noble Lord Carrington, and some of his friends, I am among the offenders who are life peers, let me say with all the emphasis at my command that I came to your Lordships' House to do a job and I intend to do it.'

Another prominent Tory peer immediately rose to say that Lord Carrington's remarks had been misconstrued and that he in fact 'welcomed life peers most strongly and considered that their introduction had brought a great improvement to the House'. This did not quite mollify Desmond. He did not easily forgive slights, real or imagined, and Carrington's intervention still rankled when their paths crossed thirteen years later.

The fact was, however, that at this point in his career Desmond was a little too mindful of his duties as a working peer and too eager to make his views known. He was also too slow to adapt to the relaxed attitudes of the Upper House or, indeed, the upper classes. He may have risen socially, but he had brought the eager-beaver ways of the

Jewish bourgeoisie with him, and eagerness was not an admitted virtue among the English political elite.

Nevertheless, he was back on his feet again some three weeks later on the Race Relations Bill, reiterating the points he had voiced previously. That was an issue on which he could not possibly remain silent, but nearly a year elapsed before he was heard again. The occasion was the Decimal Currency Bill.

He mentioned in passing that his telegraphic address was Ellessdee, but he had no sentimental attachments to the old currency and felt that it was only sentiment which had induced the decimalisation board to retain the sixpence as a 2½ pence coin. It would, he thought, introduce an unnecessary complication to the system and urged that it should be abolished. His advice was rejected, but the coin did in fact fall out of circulation a few years later and died of its own accord. Desmond took no pleasure in saying, 'I told you so,' but he was often proved right by events.

On 11 June 1969 he spoke on the economic effects of technological change, a subject of which he had made a special study and which had led him to launch the Foundation on Automation and Employment. Computers, he said, were rapidly eliminating paperwork and becoming ubiquitous: 'By the beginning of the 1980s, we shall experience million-word desk-size or even briefcase-size computers using laser memories. Books and libraries as sources of factual material will be superseded by computers by the mid-1980s. Around the same time, we can also expect that doctors, and perhaps also other professionals, will have terminals as part of their equipment, so that doctors can plug into a computer network for diagnosis and other information.' This is precisely what happened.

Production, he said, would come to depend more on capital and less on labour and would have serious effects on the distribution of wealth. As it was, about a third of personal wealth was owned by only 1 per cent of the population, while the top 9 per cent owned 71 per cent, and he believed that as a result of automation the disparity between rich and poor would grow wider. The only way to narrow the gap was to give workers a share in the equity of the companies they worked for.

He claimed that in a minor way he had pioneered the process through his Trades Union Unit Trust, and urged the Government to adopt it on a national scale, and to make sure that multinationals, which were taking over large parts of British industry, would also be required to adopt it.

He returned to the subject a year later in July 1970. Labour was out of office by then, but the fact that he now spoke from the opposition benches did not affect his line of argument or even the tone of his contribution. He again warned of the social and economic problems which would arise out of the increasing pace of automation and urged the Government, the trade unions and the Confederation of British Industry to come together in a full-scale conference, which would have, among other things, the aim of establishing a new Centre for Employment Studies.

He also called on the Government 'to combat the challenge of inequality which now confronts us'. There had, he said, been too much concentration on how to increase wealth and too little on how to share it. And he went on: 'The share of labour in a rising national income will fall, and unless employees acquire claims in the increased property income there is clearly a grave risk of alienation and aggravated conflict between the propertied and employed classes in advanced capitalist societies.' Here too he was proved right.

Five years passed before he intervened in a debate again, and this time it was on multinational corporations. He

25. Taking his seat
in the House of
Lords, 1967, with
his sponsors Lord
Robens (left) and
Lord Carron,
Chairman of the
Bank of England

26. With Harold
Wilson in the 1970s

27 and 28. These portraits of Joseph and Rivka Eisen were painted by Willie Apap in Tel Aviv in 1976

29. Close family friend Theodore Kheel (facing camera) and his daughter

30. Bronia's brother, Menachem, who received a blessing at his wedding as promised by the Belz Rebbe

31. Desmond at his zenith, painted by Willie Apap

32. Bronze busts of Desmond and Bronia by Winston Apap. The painter and the sculptor were brothers

33. Cartoon by Sallon, 1978

34 and 35. Desmond's charitable work often allowed him to indulge his sense of fun. Above he is seen playing with some of the orphaned children from Norwood and (left) at an HHI convention where eccentric headwear seems to be *de rigueur*

36. In more formal mood: Bronia, Desmond and Her Majesty Queen Elizabeth at a Norwood function in 1989

37. Desmond was proud to serve on the Board of the Chevening Trust which oversaw the restoration of this historic house

38. His various political and business interests involved a busy social round, with Bronia always at his side. Here they attend the dinner of the British Association of Hotel Accountants in 1981

39. Desmond in the 1980s

40, 41 and 42. A renowned public speaker, Desmond was invited to conferences all over the world: here he toasts the guests at an HHI conference in Japan in 1985; relaxes with Theodore Kheel at a conference for the Foundation on Automation and Employment in New York; and addresses an HHI conference in Jerusalem in 1986

43 and 44. Speaking
in New Zealand; and
with Charles Forte in
the late 1980s

45 and 46. Bronia's daughter-in-law Maude and son Frank

47. On holiday in Zurich in 1992

opened by declaring his interests. He was a professional adviser to the Total Oil Company and Chairman of the Executive Committee of the European Regional Division of Horwath & Horwath International, which had interests in over forty countries. Multinationals, he said, were being used as scapegoats in political debate. Most of them, he believed, brought many benefits to the country through technological innovations and new industrial relations techniques, such as those pioneered by the Esso refinery at Fawley. Governments, he said, 'should beware of discouraging the geese which lay the golden eggs; both may become scarce rather quickly'. Hostility to multinationals, he felt, was a symptom of an isolationist tendency in British life.

He returned to the subject again in a debate on the referendum on entry to the European Union. Although the decision to hold a referendum was made by Labour, he viewed it with misgiving as 'an example of a very unwise decision reached through ordinary democratic procedure. It has imported into Parliament a thoroughly dangerous and unnecessary precedent.'

His work for the trade union movement, he continued, had in itself made him something of an internationalist, and he believed that workers of the world should indeed unite. European trade unionists, he said, wanted us to join the Common Market and he was sorry to see that so many British unions were apparently against it: 'We cannot allow ourselves to adopt an isolationist position, however superficially attractive it appears to be, at this juncture of our history. We must give the young people of this country a purpose for living. If this is confined to one of "Keep Britain for the British" and "We must be masters of our own destiny", then we can expect selfishness to characterise not only our international relations but also, increasingly, aspects of our national and social life. When this happens culture and civilisation diminish.'

By then his interventions were becoming rare and he made his last speech in the Lords in December 1982. It is unlikely that he would have spoken even then but for the tabling of new EEC regulations which were of immediate concern to the accountancy profession. He was specially concerned about the effects of the regulations on small businesses, with whose problems he was particularly familiar and which he tended to regard as the backbone of the economy.

He complained that the regulations were too demanding as it was, and that accountants were required to provide masses of information which their clients did not need, which the Registrar of Companies did not want, which the Inland Revenue did not seek and which loan creditors, in the main, did not demand. The brief had been prepared for him by Stoy, Hayward, but he had made his own additions and it was a spirited intervention which met with support on all sides of the House.

In all, apart from minor interventions, he made fifteen speeches in the course of his career, most of them in his first year or two as a peer. If one re-reads them, one finds few felicities of expression; even when he tried to be light-hearted, he did not always succeed. He also read his speeches, which was a further handicap, and though he was liked and admired, the bars of the House did not empty when he rose to speak. Yet he spoke with authority, compassion, sincerity and insight. There was a solid substance to his words, and his speeches on the pace and repercussions of technological change were a particularly valuable contribution to debate. He was a man with vision and many of his prognostications were confirmed by events. Moreover, though he was a Labour peer speaking from the Labour benches, he was always his own man, or, as he said in the course of a debate in 1969, 'In your Lordships House I speak from the Government Benches, but I hope and believe it is recognised that I am usually capable of expressing a frank and politically unprejudiced view.'

It was, and it added to the value of his interventions. As he had said in 1968, 'I came to your Lordship's House to do a job and I intend to do it,' and he did it with dedication and vigour.

When he became President of Horwath & Horwath International in 1975, he and Bronia had to spend a good part of the year out of the country. Though he still made the occasional appearance in the House, he no longer felt induced to speak. He was grateful for his peerage, but he clearly felt that all his hard work on various public bodies and in the Lords had merited further recognition. When he was disappointed by both Wilson and Callaghan, he more or less clammed up.

By the time he finally retired from HHI in 1984, he was seventy-one and in failing health. Although he attended the House almost every day, he felt that he had done his bit, had said everything he had to say, and was more disposed to listen than to speak. In that respect he became a fairly typical member of the Upper House. When his voice was finally stilled, the tributes to his work were many and warm.

Lord Jay, a former President of the Board of Trade wrote:

Desmond Hirshfield was one of those friends and colleagues whose reliability one could rely on over a long period of years. His helpfulness endeared him ever more deeply to many of us in all sorts of ways. His advice on apparently insoluble dilemmas was also almost invariably successful. And there must be more than one society today supporting a good cause which could hardly have survived without his help and advice. Let us remember Desmond as possessing both a keen intelligence and a kind heart.

Lord Longford, an old friend, remembered Desmond as 'an impressive figure in the Lords in personality and style of speech. He made many appreciated contributions.'

Lord Healey, a former Chancellor of the Exchequer, recalled:

> I first came across Desmond Hirshfield when he introduced the Labour movement to the advantages of investing in equities by setting up the Trades Union Unit Trust. His concern with the welfare of working people was illustrated again when he established the Foundation on Automation and Human Development the following year, which recognised the future importance of computer technology in British industry while seeking to give timely warning of its effects on employment.
>
> As an accountant by profession with an unassuming personality, he was sometimes underestimated by those who did not realise how much he had done for Britain, and the Labour movement in particular; yet he was a brilliant chairman and a witty and persuasive speaker. Like all who knew him, I shall miss him greatly.

The reference to Desmond's 'unassuming personality' was perhaps a bit wide of the mark. He was a different person on different occasions and in different company, and he may have seemed almost retiring in the presence of someone as forceful and ebullient as Healey. His very presence, however, was commanding.

Lord Cledwyn of Penrhos, a former Labour Leader in the Lords, recalled Desmond's associations with Wales and believed that had he stayed in Wales, he might have become an MP. This was unlikely, for while Desmond was a loyal supporter of the Labour Party, he was not really a political animal and never cared for the turmoil of the hustings or the scoring of political points.

Perhaps the most telling tribute came from Lord Graham of Edmonton, the Labour Chief Whip in the Lords:

> Desmond Hirshfield crowned a most successful career in service, both to the Labour Party and to the nation, when he was elevated to the House of Lords. He used his position for more than ten years to speak out strongly on issues such as Race and Immigration. During the time I knew him as Chief Whip, he was a most assiduous attender, speaking rarely in public but always available to give colleagues the benefit of his long experience. He undoubtedly was the epitome of what was hoped for in the creation of Life Peerages, and his contribution to public life cannot be overestimated.

9

A Working Peer

Once Desmond became a peer he was snowed under with duties. His secretary recalls: 'Things did become exciting then, not that they were dull before, but it was a different sort of excitement. Phone calls from Downing Street, the Foreign Office, the Home Office, the Treasury, Buckingham Palace and any number of important visitors.' She began to feel that she was no longer merely running an accountancy office but something like a Chancellery with Norwich House as an annex to the corridors of power.

Whenever there was a public job to be done, and done well, Desmond's name came readily to mind. He was a thoroughly professional accountant, efficient and painstaking, a good draughtsman, economic with time and words, pleasant to work with and keen, and he soon became one of the action men of British public life. He also knew how to juggle a full timetable, for no matter how busy he seemed, he always found time to take on something new. He liked to be in demand and over-extended, and at one time or another he served on more than a dozen government boards, committees of inquiry and other bodies; in a sense he received his peerage not only for services rendered but in anticipation of services he would render. His career was to show that the honour was well-earned, even if his hopes for further honours were to be disappointed.

In 1968 he was invited by an old friend, Anthony Greenwood, the Minister of Housing and Local Government, to serve on the Board of the Northampton New Town Development Corporation. The new town was not strictly speaking new at all but an extension of Northampton, a charming medieval county town in the south-east Midlands situated in the Nene Valley, which Daniel Defoe had described as 'the handsomest and best built town in all this part of England'. It was famed for its output of leather goods and was to shoes what Bradford was to wool and Manchester to cotton. In 1965 it had a population of about 130,000 and it was proposed that about 70,000 people, mostly from the London area, should be moved into the extension without seriously affecting the character of Northampton itself. The two aims seemed to be mutually exclusive, but Desmond and his colleagues somehow managed to reconcile them.

Nearly £330 million was earmarked for the scheme, which involved the construction of over 20,000 homes, as well as factories, shops, schools and community centres on a site of some 6,000 acres.

The Chairman of the Board was Sir William Hart, a distinguished civil servant and former Secretary-General of the Greater London Council. Desmond was Deputy Chairman. The Board included seven other members, mostly drawn from local government. The Board worked in a part-time capacity and its initial tasks were to recruit full-time staff and to ensure that government guidelines were followed. There was a great deal of preliminary planning and consultation involved and work on the actual site did not begin until 1970.

The shoe industry was in sharp decline by the 1960s, and Desmond and his colleagues worked hard to attract new industries – in electronics and light engineering – to the area. Desmond's wide business connections proved particularly useful.

Much of the land was acquired by compulsory purchase, and while land-owners had to be assured a fair price, they were not allowed to benefit directly from the enhanced values resulting from the scheme. Desmond was closely involved in working out an intricate compensation plan.

He was not afraid of getting his hands or boots dirty, and travelled frequently to Northampton to see how far developments on site were conforming to the plans on paper and to assure himself that contractors were keeping to schedules. He could be firm without being abrasive, but where standards fell below his expectations he had little hesitation in giving vent to his displeasure.

This was a particularly busy period of his life and Bronia recalls frequent journeys up the M1 in his red Rolls-Royce. 'It was exciting to see a whole town growing up, homes, shops, factories, schools among the fields and meadows. The whole place seemed to grow before your eyes, and Desmond was proud of his share in the work. He was brought in as an accountant, but by the time he finished he was an expert in town planning. He was learning all the time.'

In 1976 he was compelled to stand down because of other commitments. By then, the project had taken clear shape and had attained its own momentum. It was completed in 1985 and Northampton New Town, which had been totally integrated with the old, was widely regarded as a model of its sort.

During part of this period Desmond was also a member of the Central Advisory Water Committee and the National Committee for the Unmarried Mother and her Child, Treasurer of the United Kingdom Committee of the United Nations Children's Fund (UNICEF), on the Committee on Consumer Credit and a member of the Court of Governors of the London School of Economics. He also served on a number of Board of Trade inquiries into commercial malpractice and the Iron and Steel Arbitration Tribunal. In 1972 he was appointed by the Conservative Government to report on the monopolistic pricing practices of the nationalised steel industry.

Before he left his office in the evening, Mrs Arkell would provide him with a list of five or six different meetings in five or six different venues which he would have to attend the next day, occasionally with train timetables attached. And that was on a quiet day. He liked to spend his evenings with Bronia, but sometimes he had meetings even then. What was remarkable was not so much the unhurried manner with which he coped with them all, but his ability to absorb the mass of papers which every meeting involved. Whatever the occasion, he arrived carefully briefed.

He was associated for a time with the Prices and Incomes Board, and was impressed with the dedication and skills of the permanent staff. When the Board was wound up in 1971, he and Lord Robens set up MLH, a management consultancy to make use of their talents. The firm was an almost immediate success and from modest beginnings built up a list of clients which included the Midland Bank, Guy's Hospital, United Glass and Rockware Glass, British Steel, British Leyland, the Central Electricity Generating Board and the National Water Council. It was a signal example both of Desmond's eye for an opening and his eye for talent. In 1981 MLH was taken over by Stoy, Hayward.

The decade after Desmond was raised to the peerage was the busiest and, in some ways, the happiest of his life. In 1975 he was invited by Wilson to serve on the Top Salaries Review Body. The appointment was unpaid. The Review Body had been established in 1971 to determine the salaries paid to the higher judiciary, senior civil servants, members of the boards of nationalised industries and senior officers in the armed forces.

Salaries in the public sector were never as high as those in the private sector, for, apart from other considerations, they usually came with greater security and carried the prospect of honours. But they still had to be high enough to assure an adequate flow of top talents into top jobs. At the same time, the awards made to top people – which often provoked banner headlines – affected the expectations of everyone else, and though the sums in the round were not large, the awards had a serious effect on the Government's wages policy as well as the whole economy. Balancing such conflicting factors called for the wisdom of Solomon, but the TSRB appears to have carried out its duties to the satisfaction of both the Government and top people. It has since acquired permanent status and is now known as the Senior Salaries Review Body.

Desmond, in spite of the many demands on his time, served for three successive periods under three different Prime Ministers – Wilson, Callaghan and Thatcher – at a time of particular economic stringency. He finally stood down in 1984.

In 1975 he joined the Chevening Trust, which was in some respects possibly the most demanding of all his public jobs, but the one which gave him the most satisfaction and pleasure. 'He loved Chevening and everything about it, the house, the grounds, the people,' says Bronia; 'so did I, but it was a love affair with an unhappy ending.'

Chevening, near Sevenoaks in Kent, was the country seat of the Stanhope family and had been left to the nation by the seventh Earl. By the Chevening Estate Act of 1959 it came under the direction of the Lord Privy Seal, who served as Chairman of the Administrative Trustees. Desmond was appointed Vice-Chairman of the Trust and Chairman of its Finance and General Purposes Committee. Under the terms of the Act, the Prime Minister has the responsibility of nominating the occupant of Chevening, and from 1974 to 1980 it was the Prince of Wales.

Chevening is one of the stateliest of the stately homes of England. Originally a three-gabled house with a red roof and belfry, it was extensively rebuilt and enlarged in the seventeenth century to a design attributed to Inigo Jones. It was acquired by the Stanhopes in 1717, and they enlarged it further.

The house, which stands in about 3,500 acres of ground, is steeped in history and has associations with the Earl of Chesterfield, William Pitt the Elder and the Younger, and Lord Rosebery, who described it as 'paradise'. It was also the home for a time of Lady Hester Stanhope, the unconventional eldest daughter of the third Earl, a traveller who was fascinated by Arab life. She settled in Lebanon and, with her commanding personality, virtually treated it as a private fief; she was eventually buried there.

The house, flanked by pavilions, stands at the end of a long, winding drive. As one ascends an incline, it suddenly comes into view, its magnificent façade beautifully reflected in an ornamental lake. As one enters the hall, one is greeted by the Great Staircase, a magnificent structure made of deal and cased with Spanish oak. Supported at five points only, it sweeps upwards past a wall lined with eighteenth-century muskets, pistols and bayonets, acquired by the second Earl.

Family portraits by Gainsborough, Romney, Kneller and other line the walls of the dining-room and state-rooms. The music-room is lined with tapestries presented to the first Earl in 1708 by Frederick I of Prussia, and five rooms contain a library of more than 20,000 books, some of them dating to the earliest years of printing.

The grounds include acres of intricate shrubberies, exotic flower beds and a kitchen garden, which provided not only the usual fruits and vegetables for the household but grapes, figs, nectarines and peaches.

The building and its contents had fallen into considerable decay and the grounds were overgrown, but the bequest included a generous endowment so that the Trustees could undertake an immense scheme of repairs and restoration. The first stage was completed in 1973, and a small staff was appointed for the management of the house and its contents, the provision of household services for the occupant and his guests, the upkeep of the gardens and the routine maintenance of the estate properties.

By the time Desmond became Chairman of the Finance and General Purposes Committee, the second stage of the renovations was in progress. Working closely with the administrator of the estate, Major-General Sir John Graham, he supervised the development costs as well as the management of the estate itself.

The work appealed to him on several grounds. First there was the house itself. He and Bronia had visited many of the stately homes and most of the great art collections of Europe, but at Chevening he was not merely a visitor but one of the custodians. As the renovations progressed and the house emerged in its full splendour, he could feel that he was making a modest contribution to a major work of art.

His association with the Labour Party had gained him a certain eminence within what might be called new England.

Chevening brought him into contact with old England. While the Prince of Wales was in residence Desmond was virtually a member of the royal household.

He was essentially an urbanite, and though very English in his ways, lacked the Englishman's sentimentality about country life and had no taste for country living. He was at one point offered a small cottage on the estate for a mere £13,000, but it was too rustic for his tastes and, to the eternal regret of Bronia, he turned it down, though if his resources had run to it he might have settled for something like Chevening itself. As it was, he could enjoy all its charm without carrying any of its expense. He gloried in the place and approached it with almost proprietorial pride.

An army of the best craftsmen in the country, using the finest materials, was assembled to carry out the necessary work. It fell to Desmond to reconcile the demands of the perfectionists with the limitations of his budget and to keep costs under firm control. To an extent, Desmond the aesthete was in conflict with Desmond the accountant – as they were in his own domestic life – and in the main the latter predominated.

He found congenial company in his fellow trustees, who included Lord Cornwallis, the Lord Lieutenant of Kent; Robin Leigh-Pemberton, Governor of the Bank of England; and Dr Roy Strong, Director of the Victoria and Albert Museum. He built up a particularly close relationship with Leigh-Pemberton. Sir John Graham kept them in touch with developments, and they would meet at Chevening once a month to see how far and how fast the work was progressing, though Desmond would go down from time to time on his own to cope with problems as they arose. When, for example, any new acquisitions were proposed, he would not only have to be satisfied that they would not strain the budget but would sometimes haggle with the vendors to lower the price. He would on occasion even function as site foreman to make sure that the building schedules were being met, and no detail was too small to escape his attention, and could at times be seen bending down with some difficulty to pluck the odd blade of grass which had intruded amidst the raked gravel.

As an accountant he was immediately concerned with the effects of the tax laws on the estate. Under the Chevening Estate Act, it was intended that Chevening should be a tax-free trust. Under the 1975 Finance Act, however, no specific exemptions were made for Chevening and Desmond entered into prolonged negotiations with the Chancellor of the Exchequer, Dennis Healey, to keep Chevening free of what might have been a crippling burden. He succeeded in having the exemptions restored.

He was also concerned that the trust, which had limited resources, should not be burdened with any additional costs which might arise, and he sent the Lord Privy Seal a list of the extras he had in mind:

1. The charges for all telephone calls incurred within the House of and above the minimum to be agreed, and the cost of installing and renting any additional equipment.
2. Household laundry charges.
3. Food, drink, catering services and personal domestic requirements.
4. Domestic staff services beyond those already provided by maintenance staff employed from time to time by the Trustees.
5. Any important damage to the House or contents and contiguous outbuildings.
6. Any additional expenses incurred in the running of a kitchen garden.

The Trustees are prepared to pay the full costs of gas, electricity and heating oil, but reserve the right to review this in the light of substantial increases in consumption or fuel prices.

There could be no better illustration of Desmond's tight hand on expenditure (including his own), his tendency to cope with problems before they arose and his extraordinary eye for detail, but, of course, they made great demands on his time.

He constantly picked the brains of the experts and spent long hours watching the artists, craftsmen and landscape gardeners at work. Chevening to him was not only a source of pleasure but an education, and he gradually became something of an expert himself. However, the joys he derived from the place were soon to be cut short.

Trustees were appointed for a period of three years. His first term was renewed, and he had nearly completed his second when he was asked if he would be prepared to stay on for a third. He readily accepted, but then a few weeks later he explained that he would be unable to continue after all. He did not say why, but Bronia believes that one of the reasons was the appointment of Sir Ian Gilmour as Lord Privy Seal. Gilmour was vehemently pro-Arab and anti-Zionist and, in the eyes of some Jews, an anti-Semite. He had, however, become Lord Privy Seal in 1979 and Desmond had at first experienced no difficulty in working with him. His *volte face* was almost certainly due to the fact that the Prince of Wales had moved out of Chevening at the end of 1980 and a few months later it became known that the Foreign Secretary, Lord Carrington, had been invited to move in.

In 1968, as we have seen, Lord Carrington had observed that some life peers spoke too often, too long and on subjects outside their experience, and Desmond had been convinced that the remarks referred specifically to him. He had a good memory for slights, real or imagined and he clearly never forgave Carrington.

Moreover, the Foreign Office was pro-Arab. There was talk of PLO leader Yasser Arafat being received by the Foreign Secretary, and Desmond had visions of him and his entourage being entertained at Chevening. It was as if the Arabist spirit of Lady Hester Stanhope had come back to haunt the place. Arafat was to become more or less kosher in later years, but in 1981 he symbolised Arab terrorism in Jewish eyes. Desmond, as a proud Jew, did not relish the prospect of lining up with other Trustees to shake his hand as he arrived.

In July 1981 he wrote to Sir Ian:

As you know, I have already served as a Trustee for about eleven years and as Chairman of the FGP Committee since its formation seven years ago. To my best recollection I never missed a meeting – especially of the Committee – sometimes returning from business abroad to preside and on other occasions moving engagements to tackle urgent matters or meet colleagues' convenience.

Historic homes, fine country houses, splendid gardens or estates, antique furniture and great paintings have always been a special attraction to me. I support strongly their conservation and recognise that they are an important part of our heritage. So it was with considerable satisfaction and pride that I was privileged to become active on the Chevening Trust.

I recall vividly the state of neglect and confusion that I encountered when I went to Chevening House on my first visit. The job of rehabilitation and restoration which confronted the Trustees was enormous – and presented a considerable but exciting challenge.

With much effort and team work over the past eleven years, this very fine house is at last completely restored. And when I attended a meeting of the FGP Committee on Monday last, I had the great personal satisfaction of visiting all the rooms – now fully decorated, furnished, equipped and ready for occupation. I was personally enchanted by our achievement.

My latest visit convinced me that the Trustees' major task was completed – and that for the immediate future the foremost responsibilities of the Trustees concern Estate management – and the final stages of restoration of the amenity grounds. Therefore, clearly we have successfully reached the 'End of the Beginning'. . . .

Therefore, I have now concluded that the time has come for me to go – although I shall certainly retain a close interest in the Chevening Estate and am most willing to stay available for consultation whenever the Trustees consider it may be useful to call on me. . . .

In conclusion I would reiterate how much I have enjoyed my many years' close association with the Chevening Estate and the restoration of the House to its former glory – and how much I have enjoyed working with you and your predecessors in the high office of Lord Privy Seal.

He wrote a similar letter to the Hon. Edward Adeane, Private Secretary to the Prince of Wales, who replied:

The Prince of Wales knows what an immense effort you have put in to looking after the house and the estate and His Royal Highness will I know be very sad to hear that you are now severing your links with Chevening. I am sure, however, that this is an appropriate moment for you to make the break and I know that I am only anticipating The Prince of Wales' eventual directions when I thank you now for everything that you have done on His Royal Highness' behalf.

During the last seven of his eleven years on the Trust he was President of HHI and spent much of the year in remote parts of the globe, so that when he referred to returning 'from business abroad' he was not touching on some slight inconvenience. Mrs Arkell had by then retired, but she still worked for him part-time and kept him in touch with events at home. When there was an urgent meeting, he would sometimes fly back from Hong Kong or Singapore, while Trustees who were based in London sent their apologies, and he would sometimes arrive at Chevening only to find that there wasn't a full quorum.

He was almost certainly the most diligent member of the Trust. Thus, for example, when the conduct of a tenant was found to be not fitting with his place on the estate, it was left to Desmond to caution him. Nevertheless, as he readily acknowledged, he enjoyed every minute of his association with Chevening.

In withdrawing from Chevening Desmond must have felt that he was withdrawing from Eden, but he could comfort himself with the thought that he had made a valuable contribution to its charm and beauty. As Lord Shepherd, Labour Leader of the Lords who had made him a Trustee, observed after his death: 'He saw through the major transformation of the house as being fit for a monarch. He drove the contractors and husbanded the cash. I was glad that he lived to see the results of his endeavours.'

Mr Lawrence Banks, a fellow Trustee, wrote to him on 13 October 1981, shortly after he stood down:

Dear Desmond,
    At last Friday's Chevening F & G P there was an empty seat and only then did it really come home how much we

would miss you. Ever since I have been a trustee your wisdom, tact and good sense have been a model which I can only aspire to emulate without much chance of success. The now splendid interior of the house is a triumph for which you must take great personal credit and which should give you good cause for pride. Other less tangible things are however just as important – the excellent relationship we have maintained with a multitude of people from the lowliest gardener to the most eminent in the land and above all the continuity in carrying on Lord Stanhope's wishes as I am sure he would have wished them to be carried on.

This is a personal letter of thanks but I know my colleagues feel the same way. I hope we shall see you from time to time. You can rest secure that you have left the estate and house in excellent hands.

'As you know, I was always interested in Chevening,' wrote Desmond in the course of his reply. 'In my opinion the house and grounds are very lovely and it gave me enormous personal satisfaction to see such a splendid house becoming restored to earlier glory. It is because I really loved Chevening and its environment that I willingly put so much personal effort into the work of the Trustees and their advisors.'

He continued to be associated with Chevening even after his resignation, and when he and Bronia drove through Kent on their way to France, they sometimes made a detour to visit the estate, to admire the results of the restoration and to take pleasure in the beauty of the surrounding countryside. Occasionally they would stop for tea with Sir John Graham, who would bring them up to date on developments, but by then they were outsiders. In a way it was like revisiting the scene of a long and happy love affair which had finally ended in grief.

In 1969 Harold Wilson invited Desmond to become a Government Whip in the House of Lords, which would carry with it the office of Captain of the Queen's Body Guard of the Yeomen of the Guard. He would have the rank of Minister, and it was envisaged that he would help in the work of the Department of Trade and act as government spokesman for the Ministry of Power. Given Desmond's love of tradition, the ancient associations of the office must have appealed to him immensely. He was nevertheless hesitant and wanted to know how it would affect his position as an accountant and his obligations to his partners and clients.

In November 1969 Wilson spelt out the matter in detail:

As I told you, the basic principle involved is simply that Ministers must so order their affairs that no conflict arises, or appears to arise, between their private interests and public duties – a quotation from the manual which is supplied to all Ministers on taking office. It is a sound principle and self-evidently right; and all Ministers are required to observe it strictly. What it means in practical terms is clear as far as directorships are concerned; they should be given up (as also should any shareholdings which are likely to expose an individual to the risk of being tempted to subordinate his public duties to his private advantage).

Partnerships are rather more difficult. And here we have tended to regard the basic principle as satisfied if an individual, on becoming a Minister, dissociates himself wholly from the day-to-day running of the firm's affairs, without dissolving the partnership. Equally, he need not feel precluded from continuing to offer advice in matters of family trusts, guardianship and so forth; but as regards the daily running of the firm he should play no active part.

If your obligations to your partners enable you to

arrange matters in this way, that would clearly be the most satisfactory outcome. It need not, I think, preclude you from continuing to receive profits from the firm, if you so wish.

But you might like to consider an alternative, an arrangement whereby, on becoming a sleeping partner, you would receive from the firm not your proportionate share of the varying annual profits but simply a fixed sum which would not be directly related to the profits of any particular year and would constitute, as it were, the firm's recognition of the work which you have done for them in the past and the value of your name to them.

If I can offer you any further help, please let me know. But I hope this letter may have sufficiently clarified the position to enable you to accept the offer which I made you.

Yours,

Harold

The effort which Wilson made to accommodate Desmond's needs was a measure of the value he attached to his ability. But, after further consideration, Desmond felt compelled to say 'No'.

Bronia was in two minds about the whole situation. On the one hand, she would have liked to see him at the heart of government, attired in the full panoply of office, exercising power where he had previously exercised only influence. She was also convinced that it would have given new scope for his abilities and that he would have emerged as a statesman of the first rank. However, they had so little time together as it was that she felt a little afraid that once installed in office she would see hardly anything of him at all.

He was possibly to regret his decision and in 1976, when Wilson, after four elections and three periods in office, finally stood down from the Premiership, Desmond sent him a long personal letter which reads almost like a résumé of his own career:

> First of all, Harold, I always recognise that I owe much of what I have achieved in recent years to your confidence in me and over one special matter – but also in other respects. Bronia will always recall with gratitude you having recommended me to the Queen for a peerage. We shall never forget that great personal and friendly gesture of yours.
>
> But looking back, there have been other opportunities for me to serve our country and Party which I believe you initiated.
>
> I hope that I have always deserved your confidence. But I believe there was an occasion when unfortunately I let you down. That was when you offered me an office which would have put me on the Government Front Bench in the Lords. Alas, your invitation came unexpectedly and at a moment, unfortunately, when I was not ready for it. I was too involved professionally to be able to extricate myself – and had to consider possible adverse consequences for my immediate colleagues. Nor at the time could I have afforded the very considerable reduction in earnings which political office would have involved. My level of living expenses was geared to my income – and with comparatively high earnings and little capital, there would have been a domestic financial problem of considerable proportions. I was sincerely sorry to refuse your invitation at that time.
>
> Although it might be thought in view of this that I failed your confidence in me and let down the Labour Party in the Lords, I like to believe that I have partially made amends through the several other (and interesting)

jobs – insignificant as some of them might seem to be in governmental terms – which I am doing for the country and in the interests of the Labour and Trade Union movements – and which I think in several instances have resulted from your personal suggestion and recommendation.

[He then went on to list the various public duties he had undertaken, some of which he had already completed. (Curiously, he failed to mention the efforts he had put in to reorganise Wilson's private office, which had been turned down by Labour HQ in 1970.)]

During your long and arduous but historic period in Office as Prime Minister, Bronia and I have desisted from inviting you to spend an evening with us. Perhaps that was our mistake, but we always recognised that the many calls on your time left you with little free time – and that others were more entitled to share any time you had. But now all that has changed – so we shall certainly hope that Mary and you will be able to join us for dinner occasionally.

Lengthy as this letter is, I must add a few further sentences. Bronia and I have been your consistent admirers. We know that your Premiership, your service to the country, the party and mankind have been distinguished and memorable. Not only have you been in office for a record period – but you have deserved to be. You will be missed in so very many ways. But surely you merit and will enjoy a high and proud place in British history.

It is certainly true that a man in Desmond's position would have been out of pocket through accepting public office, but not seriously so. His practice was not particularly large, and not particularly lucrative, and in 1974 he earned about £40,000. In 1969 it would have been nearer £30,000. His salary as a Minister would have been about £20,000 and Wilson had suggested ways in which it could have been topped up without breaching the guidelines.

Desmond's peerage had already added to the prestige of his firm and his presence on the front bench would have added more. It is difficult to believe that if he had wanted leave of absence, he would, as senior partner, have experienced much difficulty in getting it. Therefore, it seems fairly clear that his real reasons for turning down the prospect of office had little to do with money.

The Hirshfields lived well, but not extravagantly. They had a large flat in an old apartment block, but no country house or even a cottage. They had a Rolls-Royce, but an old one. They travelled first class and stayed in the best hotels, but as Desmond had become deeply involved in the tourist industry, they could always do so at a discount, and in any case they rarely had more than one holiday a year. Bronia was always well dressed, and Desmond would buy her a special outfit on her birthday, but she bought her clothes off the peg and in sales. If anything, Desmond was the more expensive dresser, because, until the costs approached the four-figure mark, he usually had his suits hand-made, and he always wore hand-made shoes. Bronia's son was thirty-three and more or less self-supporting, so they had no dependants.

Their biggest extravagance was the scale of their entertainment, but even there they were modest. Bronia bought almost everything she needed in Berwick Street market. In any case, they no longer entertained so frequently. Thus even if Desmond had little capital, a little capital can, with a little care, be made to go a long way. And he was, after all, a professional carer.

Jonathan Bodlender, an accountant who joined HHH in the late 1960s and later became a major figure in the hotel and tourist industry, has vivid memories of Desmond's office: 'When I first worked for Desmond in the firm's premises at Norwich House in Holborn, his office gave the impression of being part Dickensian and part a family museum. . . . Just down the corridor behind the equally Dickensian reception was a photocopier. The "wet" photocopier, already becoming obsolete, was only switched on for one hour each day and a young partner such as I had to queue with other staff to make a photocopy and sign a book listing each and every copy.'

Desmond never threw his money around and, had he been so minded, he could have survived without difficulty in reasonable comfort on a Minister's salary. And, as it happens, he wouldn't have had to, for though he didn't dabble on the Stock Exchange, he did dabble in property on a fairly large scale and had built up a group of property companies which yielded a very considerable income. The management of this could have been vested with trustees.

The office, moreover, would have made him a member of the royal household, no small distinction for the grandson of an immigrant. He would also have loved all the pomp and ceremony associated with the Yeomen of the Guard, but he would have been rather less happy as a Government spokesman.

With all the authority and self-assurance which Desmond exuded, and all his experience as a public speaker, words did not come easily to him. Though he had to take part in debates, he was not a master of debate, was not particularly good at the instant riposte and would have dreaded the cut and thrust of Parliamentary exchanges, even in the restrained surroundings of the House of Lords. He enjoyed prominence, but was nervous of over-exposure and, on balance, preferred to exercise his abilities and influence behind the scenes.

In 1961 Desmond was asked by a City journalist on the

Evening Standard which party was better for investors, Conservative or Labour. 'Now you are getting on to politics,' Desmond replied. 'I have no political ambitions.'

This was perhaps not quite the case in 1961, but it may have been true by 1969. For Labour had by then moved emphatically to the left, while Desmond, until the end of his days, remained an unabashed Gaitskellite. He had already demonstrated his independence of mind in more than one House of Lords speech and he might have found it difficult to defend policies about which he had serious reservations.

By November 1969, moreover, the Government was on its last legs. Polls indicated a likely defeat in the forthcoming elections, which were confirmed by events in the following June. Desmond may have felt that the prospect of a few months in office was unequal to the problems involved in resigning from his partnership.

Yet with all that, he would almost certainly have swallowed his reservations had Wilson offered to make him a full Minister with his own department; what he did offer must have come as something of a disappointment. At fifty-six he felt too old for minor office as a side-kick to one of the less important Ministers. Given his track record – which he was at pains to describe in detail – he may reasonably have felt that he deserved better.

The letter, therefore, reads like a bid to be remembered in Wilson's resignation honours list – as well as perhaps something small for Bronia, who had spent twenty-five years wining and dining the cream of the Labour movement, harbouring their confidences, overlooking their indiscretions, laughing at their jokes, listening to their woes, applauding their successes and commiserating with their set-backs. If so, he was again disappointed. What made it worse was the fact that he had by then also been edged out of his accountancy practice.

10

HHI

———————

Hesketh Hardy Hirshfield prospered in the post-war years under both Labour and the Conservatives and attracted a growing number of clients from the hotel and catering industry. This in turn brought Desmond into contact with Horwath & Horwath International, an American accountancy group which was one of the principal specialists in this field.

HHI grew out of the vision of two Jewish Hungarian brothers, Ernest B. and Edmund J. Horwath, who had emigrated to the United States as young men in 1907. They set up as accountants in 1915 with a special interest in the hotel and catering trade and both were astounded at the wholesale waste, pilfering and downright robbery to which the entire industry was prone. Such things were not unknown in other industries, but the catering trade was particularly affected because, on the one hand, it offered greater opportunities for abuse and, on the other, it used a great deal of casual labour and could not always build up the sense of corporate loyalty one might expect from a permanent staff.

The brothers weighed up the practices and idiosyncrasies of the industry and devised a revolutionary method of cost control, which gave their clients a vivid, and sometimes startling, picture of what they were buying, what they were selling, what – if anything – they were making and what they were losing.

They had found a gap in the market, grew rapidly and opened branches in different states, but they acquired an international dimension only after the Second World War when Ivan L. de Naray, another Hungarian and a partner in their Miami office, began to contemplate Latin America as a tourist centre and brought in Juan A. Seif – who, perhaps needless to say, was also Hungarian – to open a branch in Venezuela. It proved a success, and other offices were opened in rapid succession in Mexico, Colombia and Puerto Rico.

Then de Naray hit upon a further idea. Overseas offices required a knowledge of overseas conditions which they did not always possess, a large capital outlay, which they did not always have, frequent travel and an expensive search for overseas staff. Why not set up exclusive representation agreements in various countries with well-established local accountancy firms? In 1956 Horwath & Horwath International (HHI) was born. Initially it was confined to the Americas and the Caribbean. Then, as it branched out into Israel and the Middle East, it was joined by Dan Bavly, the enterprising senior partner of Bavly Millner Rieck of Tel Aviv.

Bavly had known Desmond for many years and in 1961 had set up an international partnership with him and the American firm of Kipnis and Karchmer, which functioned briefly as Hirshfield Kipnis Bavly & Co. (International). It was Bavly who arranged the match and de Naray was immediately taken with Desmond, his vision, personality, charm, alacrity and range of contacts. Desmond, in turn, was impressed with the expertise which HHI had brought to bear on the hotel and tourism industry and the prospects which de Naray unfolded before him.

He had by then given serious thought to the social revolution which would ensue from automation and was convinced that of all the industries with which he was connected, none had the growth potential of international tourism. As a result of their meeting, he set up Horwath & Horwath (UK) as a subsidiary of HHH to provide an advisory service to the hotel, catering and tourist trade, while de Naray went on to establish similar links with France, Germany and Italy.

It soon became clear to de Naray that his own firm in America was too small to function as the flagship of a large and growing international organisation, and in 1967 Horwath & Horwath merged with Laventhol, Krekstein, Griffits of Philadelphia to become Laventhol & Horwath. The merger created one of the largest accountancy firms in America and put HHI on the map as a major international enterprise. It also gave Desmond an invaluable link with the North American market.

HHI was not a multinational but a loose association of independent companies, some large, some small, but all of them highly regarded and well established in their own particular areas, who had come together for their mutual benefit. Each member could draw on the local expertise of the others and could refer business to the others, and all could draw on the specialised knowledge of HHI in tourism, hotel management and catering.

HHI organised seminars for partners, managers and staff

and produced a large number of manuals and other publications for their guidance. It also held training courses for junior staff. HHI received a fee and a commission on any business it generated, but no one company was in any way responsible for the liabilities of the other. Nor could any member in difficulties look for help to any other except on an informal and discreet basis, because a tacit condition of membership was a sustained record not only of solvency but of success. Anyone known to be in difficulty was out. HHI meant business. It was not a friendly society.

If the growth of HHI made it necessary for Horwath & Horwath in America to find a larger partner, the very growth of the business soon made it necessary to look for a larger associate in England. Initially, there was no thought of dropping HHH, for apart from anything else they valued Desmond's ability and judgement. They therefore urged him to link up with a larger company and he approached Teddy Langton and Philip Sober, international partners in Stoy, Hayward & Co., about the possibility of a merger.

SH, founded in 1903, was about the same age as HHH; there the similarities ended. Until about 1955 they had roughly the same number of partners and personnel, and fairly similar earnings, but in the course of the next few years SH doubled in size and then doubled again until by 1974 it had twenty-four partners and a staff of 250 and was one of the top twenty accountancy firms in the UK. HHH, with seven partners and a staff of sixty, was one of the many middle-sized firms in the country, well-managed, highly regarded and successful, but not in the same league.

This was no reflection on Desmond's professional competence. While he had been active in the House of Lords and had served on the Northampton New Town Development Trust, the Chevening Trust and half-a-dozen other quangos and had become virtually a part-time member of HHH, Langton and Sober had devoted themselves exclusively to SH.

One must add that Desmond also had numerous prestigious clients, like the Labour Party, the Print Workers, the National Union of Railwaymen, the Electricians and the International Transport Workers, but prestigious clients are not always lucrative ones. If anything, the revenues which an accountant can hope for from a client are sometimes in opposite ratio to his prestige.

Desmond's position as a member of the House of Lords and an important public figure in almost daily contact with senior bankers, politicians and industrialists added a good deal to the standing of his firm, but not perhaps as much as he thought.

Small firms merge with – or rather are swallowed by – large ones all the time, but what Desmond had in mind when he approached SH was something like a marriage of equals. Langton and Sober, while appreciating all that he had to offer, felt that his terms were not acceptable or even remotely practicable. A few months later Michael Shulman and Ab Nestor of Levanthol & Horwath (Canada) took the matter up with Sober and pointed out the many benefits which would ensue from a merger. HHH had wide contacts and extensive experience in hotels and tourism. SH had numerous clients in the hotel and catering trade, including Grand Metropolitan Hotels, one of the largest hotel and catering groups in the country. They would complement each other.

At the same time, Shulman persuaded Desmond to ease his terms and in September 1974 negotiations began in earnest. Langton, a moon-faced figure with shaggy eyebrows and a neat moustache, who had been senior partner throughout SH's dramatic growth, was a tough negotiator. So was Desmond. He was one man in the drawing-room and another at the conference table, and half relished such confrontations. His affable manner disguised a grim tenacity. His eyes hardened, his mouth tightened, a harsh tone entered his voice and, if he didn't have his way, he could be tempestuous, especially when he had a weak hand. He stormed out of one meeting and then another, but always came back, as he had to, for Langton held all the aces. SH was not only the larger and more prestigious firm, but Desmond needed the merger far more than Langton. If he had not merged with a larger firm, HHI would have found a new partner, and the terms he got from Stoy, Hayward were as good as, if not better than, he was likely to get from anyone. This was in some respects the most crucial phase of his professional career.

The terms were finally announced on 20 January 1975. The Manchester practice of HHH would continue as an independent firm with its own partners, but the name would cease to trade in London. The seven partners and staff from HHH would join the new company with Langton as senior partner, while another parallel ghost partnership was formed with its own letter-heads listing Desmond as senior partner. As a public figure and a peer who was on first name terms with the Governor of the Bank of England and who numbered half the Labour Cabinet as his personal friends, he could not tolerate the thought that he could be anything less than the senior partner in Stoy, Hayward. The new arrangement, with all the paper paraphernalia, was therefore a face-saving device, but, to anyone in the accountancy world, a fairly transparent one. However, Desmond was not as concerned about the opinion of his professional associates as his political ones.

The merger also welded them into one of the major members of the HHI network, which by then comprised forty-two member firms with 109 offices in forty-four countries.

Following the merger Desmond's artistic talents were put to good use. Jonathan Bodlender and another colleague, Peter Copp, had been given responsibility for the company's new visual image and logo, but were not enthusiastic about what the public relations company had suggested. As Bodlender recalls, 'Desmond happened to come into our offices and we showed him these logos before turning to the matters we needed to discuss. Meanwhile Desmond "doodled". At the end of our discussion he gave us his doodles. These became the logos of Stoy, Hayward and Horwath and Horwath for the next fifteen years.'

Desmond's actual function in London, as in Manchester, was that of consultant and his advice was highly valued and frequently sought. He was also given a spacious and elegant office in Stoy, Hayward's headquarters in Baker Street, retained his long-standing Mrs Arkell, and still kept a few private clients, who insisted on his personal services (which they continued to do until the end of his days). But, at sixty-one his career as an accountant was effectively over. He had found a partner and lost a job.

It was not an outcome he had envisaged, but it was not entirely unwelcome. He was never particularly excited by the routines of his calling, which was one of the reasons why he was so ready to assume so many external burdens, some of which were unpaid while the rest were not particularly lucrative.

The change meant a drop in income but he was not a poor man and he could take it in his stride. He and Bronia entered upon a new phase in their lives, which lasted for more than a decade and which could be called their travelling years.

In 1971 they had moved out of Hanover Gate Mansions into a smaller but more modern, more elegant flat over-looking Regent's Park with a panoramic view of London; on a clear day they could see as far as the Surrey hills. Bronia had found the flat and had fallen in love with it. Desmond shared her feelings, and she immediately busied herself finding the furniture and furnishings to go with the new setting.

They could still entertain, and often did, but on a more modest level, for apart from anything else their small, round dining-room table could only accommodate about eight guests. They would have friends round for drinks, but they no longer served as a gilded soup kitchen for the upper echelons of the Labour movement, and had adopted a new and more restrained lifestyle.

Desmond had joined the Executive Council of HHI in 1966. At his suggestion the group was reorganised on a regional basis and, shortly after the merger with SH, he became head of the European region based in London.

Since its inception HHI had been for obvious reasons, headed by senior partners from the American firm. The first President was de Naray, who held office from 1962 to 1974 (when he became President Emeritus); the second was Victor Seidman, who served from 1974 to 1978. The third was Desmond, which reflected both the importance and size of SH, and his personal standing within HHI.

Desmond often observed that people could be divided into three groups, 'those who make things happen, those who watch things happen, and those who wonder what happened'. He was manifestly in the first group and had little patience for the other two. On assuming office he vowed to 'strive to continue the HHI tradition of making things happen, and I intend to have fun doing it'.

He did, but he also made sure that others joined in the fun. With his sense of showmanship, his theatrical zest and his feeling for gaiety, he could convert even an international convention of accountants into a cheerful and exuberant occasion. Bodlender vividly recalls Desmond's dry, even wicked, sense of humour and tells how he presided over the annual meetings of HHI with considerable style and wit.

The office was not honorific; it came with the job of Chief Executive. The salary was $100,000 (about £80,000) a year, which, given the nature of his responsibilities, was not high even by 1978 standards. His main task was to strengthen the links between the different associates of HHI, bring in new members and, where they were not up to scratch, weed out old ones.

As President, Desmond also set out to preserve and enhance the 'family' image and spirit of HHI, which, as Bodlender says, 'had been almost a club when he joined as the first member outside North America in 1962. No enquiry or request for advice from an overseas colleague, however remote the firm, was too unimportant for him to answer personally, promptly and fully. . . . His visit around the South American member firms fairly shortly after the end of the Falkland Islands' war was a "tour de force" and remains legendary in that continent.'

Bronia nearly always accompanied him on his travels, helping to entertain the wives and find out about the different ways of life in the many countries they visited. She believes that he always paid her expenses out of his pocket. Given the fact that, wherever possible, they travelled first class and stayed in five-star hotels, he would have been left with little change out of his salary. He, however, loved the job and for the next six years spent much of his time on the wing visiting the various outposts of HHI. Sometimes he would wake up in the morning without being quite certain where he had been and where he was. In 1983 alone he covered about 35,000 miles, visiting fourteen major commercial centres in ten different countries.

In July 1981, on their thirtieth wedding anniversary, he wrote to Bronia in what can only be described as a mood of exultation: 'The first 10 years were great. The second 10 wonderful – and the third 10 fantastic. So now for lots more years in happiness, peace and good health – TOGETHER.'

He and Bronia rarely ate on planes, if only to avoid jet-lag, but they made an exception for Concorde, not only because it was particularly fast but because the fare was particularly splendid. Desmond, who was an expert on such things, thought of it as one of the best dining-rooms he had come across, even if it was rather cramped.

Member firms of HHI were expected to be competent and energetic. If they were deficient in either respect, he would encourage them to do better. If they failed, he would weed them out. It was a painful duty but a necessary one, for the poor performance of one firm could undermine the standing of the rest, and Desmond could be ruthless if the occasion demanded. However, he made a detailed study of every country he visited – its history, geography, political system and economic prospects – and made allowances for the particular environment in which member firms had to operate and the special problems they faced.

'I don't barge in expecting people to be conducting themselves in accordance with English and American circumstances,' he said. 'In some parts of the world, the laws have not required companies to provide audited accounts, so there is a great deal of tax avoidance. Some businesses produce three sets of figures: one for themselves, one for the Government, one for shareholders.' He did not explain how auditors coped with them all. 'Elsewhere,' he added, 'accountants cannot get professional indemnity insurance. When I offered to get them covered outside through Lloyds I was told, no thanks, we don't have claims in our country because people know we have insufficient money to pay material compensation. If we were insured people would sue us.' He was later to discover that even very large companies in highly developed countries could sometimes succumb to local difficulties through the very fact that they were amply covered and insured.

He was particularly anxious to help small and struggling firms and developing countries. He would invite them to seminars and send over experts from America or Britain to guide them. If their problems were particularly intractable, he would try to sort them out himself. In the main, however, his job was to attract new members, retain the loyalty of old ones, enhance the image of HHI and give it a closer sense of family. He succeeded at every level.

When de Naray began to build up HHI, he travelled tirelessly to recruit likely firms. By the time Desmond took over, they had to apply for membership and he would vet them to see if they were up to scratch. If they were efficient but small, he would urge them to do what he had been forced to do himself and merge with other firms in their locality. They would then serve a term of probation as correspondents before being accepted as full members.

He also sent detailed reports to head office on every firm and every country he visited. Some of them ran to forty or fifty pages and were carefully considered and cogently argued. The skill with which they were drafted suggested that he was a lawyer at heart rather than an accountant, which was indeed the case. Desmond excelled at report-writing and was as fastidious in the written word as he was in his appearance. Jonathan Bodlender remembers the advice and help Desmond gave him as a young partner when he first had to draft professional reports. He recalls how the words 'we feel' disappeared from Horwath reports 'from the moment Desmond rather acidly enquired of me with what did I feel it. Since then Horwath consultants have expressed opinions, not feelings.'

Membership was not cheap. Smaller firms earning less

than $10 million a year paid 0.05 per cent of their gross net fees, with a minimum of $500; larger ones paid 0.10 per cent. On top of that firms paid a premium of 13 per cent on the first $50,000 earned through work referred to them by other members of HHI and 15 per cent on any sums beyond that. In spite of this, the family grew year by year, as did the volume of business. By the time Desmond retired as Executive Director in 1986, HHI was one of the thirteen largest audit groups in the world, employing over 7,000 personnel in 217 offices in 75 countries, with a fee income of over $200 million.

It was represented everywhere from Andorra to Zimbabwe and, although it was well-known that most of the leading figures in HHI were Jewish and that it had three associates in Israel, it also had offices in Egypt, Saudi Arabia, Jordan, Lebanon, Yemen, Kuwait, Bahrain, Oman, Abu Dhabi and Dubai. Desmond visited several of the Middle East offices fairly regularly, and the fact that he had business interests in Israel and was on the board of one of its largest banks (Bank Hapoalim) never affected the warmth with which he was received. Such visits, however, sometimes had to be arranged discreetly and when HHI published a list of associates it added a footnote: 'At the request of certain member firms in Arab countries, their firms have not been included in this listing.'

Desmond liked to play down the importance of his title and claimed that it meant nothing in England, which was not quite the case. It certainly meant a lot to him and Bronia, and meant a great deal in America and the Commonwealth countries, where he was always billed as 'The Lord Hirshfield'. It was an accurate designation, but it somehow gave the impression that he was a lord among lords, and his visits, whether to some obscure little outpost or to a major commercial centre, nearly always caused a stir. His very presence, tall, lordly, dignified, with Bronia, diminutive but dazzling, at his side, excited a sense of occasion, and they nearly always got VIP treatment. He kept the Foreign Office, where he had extensive contacts, informed of his movements, and they were often received by the British Ambassador or Consul, or local dignitaries. His opinion was widely sought, especially in countries anxious to expand their tourist trade, and he was frequently interviewed in the press, on the radio and on television.

He preached the same message wherever he went, albeit in different words. Automation, he argued, was reducing the working week and the working year, and would continue to reduce it at an accelerated pace, even in less developed areas of the globe. People – where they were actually employed – would be spending less time at work and more time at play, and would be enjoying larger incomes, so that no industry had the growth prospects of the leisure industry, which even then was second in size only to the fuel and power industry. He did not claim that the development was a healthy one, and readily confessed that he was not cheered by the prospect he saw ahead, but felt that it was inevitable. In fact, he made it clear that he drew comfort from the thought that he would not live to see his visions fulfilled.

He did not like to beat about the bush and could indulge in straight-talking, even in countries where candour was not readily encouraged or appreciated. In Indonesia, for example, he told a press conference that while the country had a pleasant climate, magnificent scenery, a friendly people and a host of cultural and historic attractions, it had no hope of building up a large tourist trade while visitors were subjected to endless queues at passport control and prolonged searches in customs.

Though HHI had special, perhaps unique, expertise in

tourism, it also had interests in countries where tourism enjoyed a low priority, or was even discouraged. For example, it was invited to organise the catering arrangements in a vast new government hospital in Saudi Arabia. It also became increasingly involved in private health care, or 'the hospitality industry', as it came to be known.

There were the inevitable public banquets and Desmond was invariably asked to speak, usually on accountancy or finance, not the most exciting of subjects, even to other accountants and financiers, but he avoided florid expressions, was always pertinent and usually brief, with unexpected bursts of wit. He had a soft voice, but his commanding presence added power to his words.

However, his sense of humour was also present on these occasions and his speeches often contained a relevant joke or two. Theodore Kheel, the distinguished American lawyer, recalls one dinner in New York when Desmond was about to speak to top American labour leaders on behalf of the British Foundation on Automation and Employment. During dinner the microphone went dead: 'There was an awkward pause and some restlessness in the audience before the microphone came on. Desmond eased the tension by inquiring as his first words, "Can you hear me, Mother?"'

As we have seen, his mother had been a well-known variety artist before her marriage, and Desmond did not need much encouragement to display the theatrical side of his character. For example, on one occasion while entertaining some American friends at Madame Patachoux, an expensive club in Montmartre, Paris, he discovered that it did not accept cheques or credit cards and he did not have enough cash to pay the large bill. He therefore paid for his supper by joining in the cabaret: he dressed up as Toulouse-Lautrec and went down on his knees to perform his favourite party trick – smoking a cigarette inserted in his navel. Kheel also witnessed Desmond doing this at one of his own parties and took a photograph of this 'unique performance', which became one of Kheel's prized possessions.

Kheel has written that Desmond 'was always ready for fun and frivolity' and could be 'the life of the party'. This side of Desmond's character was given expression in his membership of the Saints and Sinners Club, an exclusive, if raffish, assembly of up-market Bohemians, successful men about town who met every month or two at the Savoy Hotel, or some equally expensive venue, to eat splendid food, drink superb wines, smoke excellent cigars and exchange execrable jokes. He also belonged to the National Sporting Club, a rather larger and less flamboyant organisation, which held similar men-only dinners on behalf of various charities.

His clients included the British branch of the Playboy organisation and he often dined amid the bunnies of the Playboy Club in Park Lane but, though he sometimes visited the gaming rooms, he never gambled. He sometimes sported a sawn-off top-hat with a curved brim, like a Regency buck, which is possibly how he saw himself, and was prone to spasms of sheer whimsicality, as one can see from the verse which he sent Bronia in November 1981 on her sixty-sixth birthday. He may have been a bit tipsy when he wrote it, and even tipsier when he sent it:

> I come from Birmingham England,
> ¼ French, ¼ Vermouth
> and ¼ vodka and ¼ Riesling
>
> You come from great roots.
> Honest, conscientious, steeped
> in Bible and Lokshen Soup
> . . . and boiled chicken.

How wonderful you are.
How tremendous I am.
(belly and all).

From precious husband, to a precious wife,
Very fondly.

The highlight of the HHI calendar was the annual conference attended by delegates from all member firms, which inevitably included a lavish banquet and many speeches. The lingua franca was English and Desmond was often the star turn. He would often brighten his remarks with ironic observations.

'Many of us spend a good proportion of our time either preparing financial statements, or assisting others to prepare them,' he told an HHI gathering in San Francisco in 1982, 'but, I wonder, are we in fact just wasting our time? Does anyone want these financial statements? Does anyone use them? And even if there are affirmative answers to both these questions, does anyone really understand them?' These were painful questions to put to a hall full of accountants, but they not only conveyed his own misgivings on the matter, they were designed to make the audience sit up. He went on to make a plea for openness, clarity, pertinacity, precision, honesty and adaptability.

'Accountancy as a profession', he concluded, 'must be seen not only to welcome change, but also to be the instigator of change. It must be mindful of its wider professional responsibilities and, finally, it must not become a profession of technicians, but a profession trained and willing to use astute and proper judgement in all matters for which it is responsible.' It must be said that as an accountant and as a man he strove earnestly to live up to his precepts.

These annual gatherings were, at first, sacred to men. The food was good, the wine was excellent, the surroundings were luxurious, but the atmosphere was not always congenial All that changed in 1967, when wives or 'partners' were also invited, and the gatherings became more colourful, light-hearted and festive. Bronia, with her good looks, perfect dress-sense and sparkling personality, contributed hugely to the transformation. What began as an innovation soon hardened into a tradition and she became one of the ornaments of the HHI jamborees, especially after Desmond became President.

In so far as these gatherings had a practical purpose, it could have been quickly completed over a cup of coffee in some drab conference hall, but they were essentially celebrations. One had to be successful to join HHI, and stay successful to remain in it, and members came together once a year to congratulate one another and to drink (and eat) to their good fortune.

They did so in style, and the different hosts in the different countries tried to outdo each other in the splendour of their hospitality and the lavishness of their entertainment. They chose the best venues in the most attractive settings, such as the Ritz in Lisbon, Old Bookbinders in Philadelphia, a country club near Toronto, the new Art Museum in Melbourne, the Stockholm Town Hall, the Castil de Petollado near Barcelona, the Intercontinental Hotel with its Arabian nights' atmosphere on the Mount of Olives in Jerusalem, and the ancient splendours of the Castel Sant'Angelo in Rome.

Most memorable of all, however, was a banquet at the Dorchester Hotel with over four hundred guests, where The Lord Hirshfield entered in scarlet and ermine with a coronet on his head, preceded by the band of the Grenadier Guards in scarlet and busbies. The State Opening of Parliament had taken place earlier that day, which two or three of his guests had witnessed from the public gallery of the House of

Lords. 'For the benefit of those who did not witness the spectacle earlier in the day,' he said amid rapturous applause, 'I thought you might wish to see it now.' Accountancy, if not the most glamorous of callings, had its compensations.

HHI's philosophy was defined by de Naray, its true begetter, in the following terms:

> Information about our friends and associates in distant lands reminds me of how various musical instruments create the final and majestic whole – the symphony orchestra. The separate musical instruments are the various offices, staffs and types of specialised knowledge of our associate firms of Horwath & Horwath. They have already shown that by working together it is possible to combine the special timbre, tone and quality of each to produce a sweep of harmony.

To which he might have added that to get the necessary sweep of harmony, one needs a good conductor, and Desmond was one of the best. He had warmth, charm, energy, patience, insight, a ready intelligence and a capacious mind. He could get on with people from different backgrounds and cultures, spoke several languages, had wide international contacts, great personal standing and a wide range of expertise. He could also, if occasion demanded, be tough, but with all the gravitas he sometimes brought to proceedings, he also had an English taste for frivolity and knew when to let his hair down.

It is fortunate that, given the nature of his responsibilities, he and Bronia loved to travel. In the more outlying places they sometimes had to fly in ancient, shaky craft, held together by wires and string, which seemed to flap their wings, but otherwise it was a matter of first-class travel, first-class hotels, and first-class meals in first-class restaurants; though given the scale and frequency of their travels, it was perhaps inevitable that they should suffer the occasional misadventure.

In 1984 they set off on a visit to Malaysia. When they landed in Kuala Lumpur, instead of the usual embassy limousine they were met by two silent, swarthy figures in a battered car. They drove them to their hotel without a word. Bronia got out, the luggage was unloaded and, before she could turn round, they had vanished with Desmond in the back seat.

She was mystified and more than a little perturbed, but they were in a Moslem country and she presumed she was not welcome in the company of men.

She was exhausted from the journey and lay down to rest. When she woke an hour or two later, there was no sign of Desmond nor any message from him. He was by then in failing health and she was afraid that he might have been taken ill. Worse, all the stories she had read about hostages and kidnapping began to rush through her mind and she could see him as another Terry Waite chained in some dank dungeon. The more she thought about it, the more gruesome her visions became. Whatever qualities of temperament Bronia may claim to possess, equanimity is not one of them. She called the British High Commission, but, to her surprise, Desmond had not told them he was coming and they had no idea where he could be.

She was about to phone the police, but then remembered that Desmond had planned to visit the local affiliate of HHI. She called an English-speaking taxi and asked to be taken to every accountant in town. There were more than she or the driver had bargained for, each miles from the other, located in back bedrooms, basements, attics, and garden sheds. After hurtling around for about two hours, Bronia was growing desperate. The driver, in the meantime, had had enough and wanted to take her back to the hotel.

'Just one more,' she pleaded tearfully, 'one more, and then we'll go to the police.'

She finally found Desmond in a small office on the top floor of a dingy block of flats, looking as distraught as she felt. She collapsed in his arms. He had tried to call her, but the lines were out of order.

'I can laugh at it now,' she says, 'but it was no laughing matter at the time. I nearly died.'

On another occasion in Korea, they had a lunch appointment at 12.30 with the British Consul. Advised by the hotel not to hail a taxi in the street, the concierge arranged for a special car to drive them to the Consulate. The driver did not – or did not want to – understand English and began to drive them miles out into the countryside. Desmond started pointing at his watch, indicating that they were going to be late, but Bronia, realising that the Consulate could not possibly be so far outside the city, began to panic and started banging on the window. However, the driver did not respond. Then Desmond coolly took out his House of Lords' pass, which looked like a police card, and the driver immediately turned around and took them back to the Consulate. They eventually turned up for lunch at 2.15 to be met by a very worried Consul.

In 1983 HHI produced a brief history of the organisation and in a preface Desmond referred to the pleasure he took in the fact that the work which had appeared during his term as Chief Executive was drawing to a close. 'But if destiny allows,' he added, 'I hope to remain active within HHI in another capacity for a while longer and hope to witness the further development of HHI as it moves towards its first half century.'

When his first period as Chief Executive had ended after three years in 1981, it was extended by another. He then dropped broad hints that he would not be averse to a third term; these were not however taken up. Everyone agreed that he had done a marvellous job, but it was a plum job and others wanted their turn. As a mark of appreciation for his devoted services, eighteen trees were planted in his and Bronia's name in Galilee.

Tree-planting has a symbolic significance among Jews, for it suggests permanence and continuity, and the number eighteen in Hebrew symbolizes life, but it did not symbolise munificence. In fact, it was the sort of presentation one might make to a Barmitzvah boy. Had they gone to the expense of planting a Hirshfield forest in Galilee, Desmond might have been mollified, but a mere eighteen trees simply added insult to injury.

He was compensated in 1984 with the job of International President, a cumbersome title, and though it was not completely honorific it involved far fewer duties. He was having trouble with his hips by then and, as always, had difficulty with his breathing, and though he and Bronia continued to travel it was not as frequently or as extensively.

It must be said that Desmond's job as Chief Executive answered more to his love of pleasure than his love of a challenge. He did his job dutifully and he did it well, but given his talents it was not particularly demanding compared with his duties on Northampton New Town Development Corporation, or as satisfying as his work for the Chevening Trust. In essence he was little more than a super-salesman. It could be argued that as he was past retiring age and in imperfect health he was entitled to take it easy and have some fun, but he had always been in imperfect health, which had never affected his dedication to any task in hand, and he never believed that age was a barrier to advancement.

In some respects his elevation to the post of Chief Executive marked the beginning of his decline. In 1988 he retired completely; but although he was no longer involved in HHI affairs, he remained on close terms with its senior figures and was invited to its annual celebrations.

In September 1990 he and Bronia were in New York for the AGM, which was followed by a magnificent banquet at the Plaza Hotel, with much toasting, many speeches and the usual American razzmatazz. Every major figure in the far-flung HHI family was there except Boris Levine, senior partner in Laventhol Horwath, the flagship of the group and host of the evening. He eventually surfaced, grim-faced, crumpled and dishevelled. Something calamitous had occurred but very few of the guests knew what. Philip Sober, who was at the banquet and who had more than an inkling of what had happened, said it was 'like being at the final meal on the *Titanic*'.

The full story soon emerged. Laventhol Horwath was facing a welter of expensive and embarrassing suits for negligence. The sums involved were too vast and the implications too dreadful to make a salvage operation practicable; the company went into voluntary liquidation. HHI did not collapse completely, but survived in attenuated form, a shadow of the empire Desmond had helped to build. Stoy, Hayward, which had been contemplating a change of name to Stoy Horwath, immediately dropped its plans and took urgent steps to acquire a new American associate.

Desmond received the news with *schadenfreude*, though with rather more *schaden* than *freude*.

When he had retired in 1988, as a final farewell present he was given a carriage clock – the sort of gift he might have given to his partner at Christmas. An association which had given him much satisfaction and pride, and which went back nearly thirty years, ended in umbrage.

Desmond had a good memory for slights and where it was deficient he could always rely on Bronia to reinforce it. To them the collapse of Laventhol Horwath was nothing more than poetic justice.

11

Work from the Heart

Desmond was not an orthodox Jew and to the casual acquaintance, certainly in his younger years, he gave an impression of cheerful indifference to anything spiritual; but in fact he had a deeply religious streak, which may be seen from a letter he sent to a nephew on the eve of his Barmitzvah in November 1962:

My dear Graham,

The second most important date in your lifetime is now almost dawning and you are about to enter Jewish religious manhood.

I am sure you will have studied the English translation as well as the Hebrew text of this week's Sidra; and I feel that your teachers will already have explained to you its meaning and its lesson. There is an important consideration inherent in the current Sidra on which you should reflect with considerable benefit and advantage to yourself.

A Sidra is a portion from the Pentateuch read in synagogue every Saturday. A different portion is read each week and each portion raises different issues. The issue on which Desmond alighted was leadership:

> As you progress through early manhood into experience and maturity . . . you will come to recognise that no man is irreplaceable; when one person's job is done, there is always someone else to take over. So do not follow the idea which some pessimists would have us believe that all great men, great deeds and the finest eras of history are only in the past. There will be greatness in the future and in your future if you and others of your generation work hard and conscientiously. Whilst lessons are to be learnt from the past, there is much to be done and much in which to succeed in the present and the future.
>
> You are privileged to have wonderful parents who have bestowed great goodness upon you. You have a traditional Jewish background and you bear a respected name. All of these things will be of great aid to you as you steer your path through the future.
>
> May you enjoy good health, happiness and contentment. In work and in leisure may you always have faith, maintain close association with your religious environment and upbringing and grow up a respected Jew, an upright citizen of your country and the world.

Graham, now a prosperous solicitor and a leading member of his local synagogue, regarded Desmond with awe and took his letter very much to heart.

The letter was almost a sermon, but it does suggest the depth of Desmond's religious feelings and, by English standards certainly, he was a devout Jew. He also drew comfort and pride from his Jewishness.

He was too fond of good food to pay attention to the

Jewish dietary laws, but attended synagogue during the major festivals and not infrequently on Saturday mornings. He would visit the graves of his parents on the anniversary of their deaths and would say Kaddish – the memorial prayer – for them without fail. He would celebrate Passover with the traditional meal and all the traditional fare and with numerous relatives and friends around his table, and would fast every Yom Kippur until, towards the end of his life, he was stopped from doing so on doctors' orders. And even in ill-health he spent the better part of Yom Kippur in synagogue, in a prayer-shawl, with his prayer book and rarely engaging in conversation with his neighbours.

Without being particularly religious in his youth, Desmond had been a prominent and popular member of Hampstead Synagogue, and it was perhaps inevitable that in 1955 he should have been elected to represent the synagogue on the Board of Deputies of British Jews.

The Board, founded in 1760, was brought together by eminent figures in the community to present a loyal address on behalf of British Jewry on the accession of George III, and has continued to function ever since. It is mainly concerned to promote and protect the interests of the Jewish community, especially in its fight against discrimination and anti-Semitism. It also seeks to defend the interests of Israel, and for the past fifty years or more has virtually served as an arm of the Zionist movement. Its members are drawn from the various religious, welfare, cultural and social organisations which constitute the community, but it is dominated by the synagogues, and more specifically the Orthodox synagogue.

The Board contained a number of figures of real eminence, like Desmond's friend Victor Mishcon, who among other things was a former Chairman of the London County Council; Abraham Moss, a former Mayor of

Manchester; Sir Barnet Janner MP and others. But in the main it was composed of people who were highly regarded in their own parish but were little known outside it, and in essence it was a meeting-place and sounding-board for local Jewish worthies.

The organisation as a whole, however, enjoyed considerable standing both within the community and without, and the President of the Board was regarded as the lay leader of British Jewry. When Desmond joined the Board, the President was his old friend the Rev. Abraham Cohen, Senior Minister of the Singers' Hill Synagogue, Birmingham, which may have been one of the reasons why he joined it.

For a number of years Desmond applied himself to his duties with some zeal. The Board met in plenary session once a month, and in his first years he rarely missed a meeting.

In 1960, when the Board celebrated its bicentenary with a lavish banquet, Desmond brought along a substantial part of the Labour movement as his personal guests, including Lord and Lady Attlee, Alfred Robens, James Callaghan, Anthony Greenwood, Sir Vincent Tewson, General Secretary of the TUC, Bill Carron, General Secretary of the Amalgamated Engineering Union, Frank Cousins of the Transport and General Workers and Harry Douglas, General Secretary of the Iron and Steel Federation. There was some murmuring that Desmond had virtually hijacked the occasion and had converted a communal celebration into a Labour one, but this was a time when most British Jews were Labour sympathisers. Desmond's guests added to the auspiciousness of the occasion, and he helped to make the evening an outstanding success. The banquet marked the high point of Desmond's involvement in the work of the Board. By then the Rev. Cohen was dead and Desmond's interest began to wane.

In 1961 he was elected to the Board's Finance Committee. His experience of such matters and his contacts should have been invaluable, for the Board worked on a shoestring budget with expenditure regularly outstripping income and had to hold frequent emergency appeals. Desmond, however, attended only two meetings of the committee in his first year and one in his second, after which he was never seen either in committee or at the plenary sessions, though he continued to be elected year after year. He finally stood down in 1967, the year he became a peer.

The Board was not quite his scene. It was clearly too synagogual, too Zionistic, too parochial and perhaps too Jewish for his tastes, with too many people anxious to speak and too few having anything to say. It was geared for debate rather than action.

Desmond was not by nature a wordy man; he had little small talk and, though he made a point of attending meetings, he spoke only when necessary. In fact, as far as Abraham Massel, a former Executive Director of the Board, can recall, he did not generally speak; but then it is unlikely that he had strong feelings about the sort of issues which were usually raised. The mystery remains why he should nevertheless have stayed on the Board for twelve years.

There was, in fact, only one Jewish organisation which enjoyed his constant loyalties over many years and that was Norwood, which began life in 1795 as a fund for the relief of needy Ashkenazi children. The calls on the fund grew dramatically and led in 1807 to the establishment of the Jews' Hospital 'for the reception and support of the aged poor and the education and industrious employment of the youth of both sexes'.

In 1831 a parallel organisation was formed, the Jews' Orphan Asylum, 'for the maintaining, clothing, educating and apprenticing of Jewish children born in lawful wedlock, deprived of both parents, and for a limited number of one parent only'. The Orphan Asylum, which was the larger of the two, moved into spacious, purpose-built premises in Norwood, south London, in 1866. In 1876 it absorbed the Jews' Hospital, which was by then no longer concerned with the aged, and the joint organisation came to be popularly known as Norwood.

The Anglo-Jewish community at this time was still small and compact, but it doubled in size as a result of mass immigration from eastern Europe in the 1880s, and then doubled again. Where Norwood accommodated a mere 159 children in 1877, by 1912 it had expanded to take 400.

For the next fifty years Norwood continued as a residential home while the Jewish Board of Guardians (founded in 1859 and since renamed Jewish Care) looked after the welfare of deprived children living in their own homes. In 1963 Norwood took over all such responsibilities and today, under the name of Norwood Child Care, it looks after the welfare of some 4,000 Jewish children in need.

Needy children excite ready sympathies and Norwood is among the oldest of all Jewish charities and perhaps the most widely supported. It has enjoyed royal patronage since 1815, the present patron being Her Majesty the Queen, who attended a gala dinner to celebrate the 190th anniversary of Norwood in 1985. The Rothschilds were associated with the charity from its earliest years and its list of office-holders is like a roll-call of patrician Jewish families: Goldsmid, Cohen, Montefiore, Moccatta, de Mesquitta, Henriques, de Castro, Spielman, Solomon, Montagu, Behrens and, latterly, the Bearsteads (whose founding father, Marcus Samuel, was also the founder of Shell Oil). The current President of Norwood is Sir Evelyn de Rothschild.

Desmond's association with Norwood went back to 1932, when at the age of nineteen he joined the Norwood

Hampstead Aid Society, founded in 1893.

Charity is the one religious obligation which persists even among Jews who have discarded every other. There is also Jewish gregariousness. All social life, especially among the young, thus revolved round one charity or another, and groups like the Orphan Aid Society provided an opportunity not only to support a just cause but to meet the right people. Even today there are more than two dozen charity committees operating under such improbable names, as Chutzpah, Gemini, Kwids for Kids, Carousel, Scruples, Balagan, Activate, Breathing Space and Kids R Us, all raising money for Norwood.

Hampstead in the inter-war years was perhaps the most fashionable and certainly the liveliest synagogue in London, and Desmond and his friends helped to make it livelier still. The annual dinner and ball which he organised on behalf of Norwood was the premier social event of the congregation and attracted guests, young and old, from all over London. The favoured venue was Grosvenor House and, as we have seen, it was at one such ball that Desmond first introduced Bronia to his parents.

He remained active in the OAS even after he married and became its President, and in 1949, for example, it raised over £4,500 (equivalent to about £100,000 in today's terms). Such charity groups were to be found in almost every synagogue in Britain, but the Hampstead OAS was perhaps the most successful of them all. Desmond was invited to join the inner councils of Norwood and in 1960 became President of the Norwood Charitable Trust.

The Trust was the financial holding company of the organisation which, in turn, was headed by the Hon. Peter Samuel, a banker who in 1961 was to help Desmond set up the Trade Union Unit Trust. Samuel had a high regard for Desmond's abilities and persuaded him to become Joint

Treasurer of Norwood with Sydney Mason, Chairman of Hammerson, one of the largest property groups in the country. When Samuel stood down in 1976, Desmond became President of Norwood and, as such, one of the pillars of the Anglo-Jewish community.

The President had hitherto always been a member of one of the gilded Anglo-Jewish clans, someone with money and pedigree. Desmond, comparatively speaking, had neither, though by way of compensation he had a title and was the first member of the new meritocracy to hold the office. The role of President is titular and was bestowed on Desmond in appreciation of services rendered, but during his active years as Treasurer of Norwood from 1960 to 1976 the organisation underwent more – changes including two changes of address – than at any time in its history.

Where it had been concerned only with young children in its own premises, it began to look after children living at home, young adults and even single mothers, and the voluntary social workers were replaced by professionals. Special budgets had to be allocated, and Desmond kept a close eye on expenditure and was quick to pounce on inefficiency or extravagance.

At the same time, he showed a personal interest in the welfare of the children and, for example, set up a special fund to give every child his or her own Post Office savings account. Most Norwood children were trained in a craft. He encouraged them to raise their sights wherever possible and to enter the professions.

His most valuable contribution, however, lay in his fund-raising ability. Most Jewish money, especially after the Six Day War in 1967, went to Israel. Desmond never questioned the needs of Israel. He didn't even argue that charity begins at home, but he did point out that Jews were not immune from the social ills of the society around them, the broken homes, the problem families, all of which added to the responsibilities of Norwood. He was able to persuade many people not only to make generous contributions to Norwood during their lifetime but to leave generous endowments after their death. He also drew on his experience with the Hampstead Aid Society to reinvigorate the various voluntary groups raising money for Norwood, to add to their number and to give them a new sense of urgency.

In looking back over his work, one can see why Norwood engaged his energies in a way that the Board of Deputies did not. The Board talked about problems, Norwood coped with them. Desmond was essentially a man of action, though the fact that he was childless himself may have given him a special interest in the welfare of children.

Desmond's feeling towards children and the needy can be summed up in a brief saying that he once jotted down on a notepad:

> I love the Unloved
> I will help a stranger
> I will teach children
> to grow up as man
> to face the world not in anger.

Bronia, who had worked with Desmond on the Hampstead OAS, has happy memories of the visits they used to make to the children and the garden fêtes they attended in the grounds of Norwood House: 'The ladies in elegant hats, the children nicely behaved and beautifully turned out, the young people, the bright sunshine, the lovely grounds, the marvellous company. Famous people, famous names. We all had a marvellous time. I loved it.' The children also loved Desmond, running up to him to take his hand and show him around the fête. The party, which harnessed the energies and enthusiasm of all the aid societies and which was attended by everybody who was anybody in Anglo-Jewry, formed one of the social highlights of the year. It also raised a fortune.

By the 1960s the idea of keeping children together in a large institution was no longer acceptable. Norwood House was a large and imposing edifice built in the high-noon of Victorian gothic, but though ornate without, it was bleak within. In appearance and regime it was not unlike a traditional English public school, though the accents of the children did not always go with it, and the food was probably better; but it became increasingly expensive to run and ruinously expensive to maintain. Indeed, some critics averred that it would have been cheaper to send the children to Eton, and the building was finally demolished in 1961. It was not replaced, and some children were fostered with private families, while others were moved into smaller homes, each with resident foster-parents, in north and north-west London. Old Norwood was no more, and it fell to Desmond and his colleagues to transfer the loyalties which had grown round the old establishment to the new.

In 1973 the grounds of the orphanage, Knight's Hill in south London, were sold for £1,400,000. Sydney Mason was largely responsible for clinching the deal. Desmond, as Joint Treasurer, played a leading role in the negotiations and was rather proud of the sum obtained, and for the first time in its history the organisation found itself with a large surplus on its hands. It was then that he got caught up in a controversy which was to dog him for some years.

In 1951 he had written a detailed study of Anglo-Jewish charities for the *Jewish Chronicle*, in which he complained that some charities had 'the unfortunate habit of withholding from their subscribers and even from the members of their own management committees, a good deal of information as to their assets, for the reason that in their view a disclosure of this might result in their future support and income diminishing'. Yet Desmond was not all that forthcoming about the true financial situation of Norwood, and was aghast when Mr Vivian Harris, a former Chairman of the Norwood Trust, revealed that the orphanage had been sold for £1,400,000. Desmond denounced it as a breach of confidence, though as the buyer was a local authority the figure was in fact in the public domain.

Harris also went on to argue that as Norwood was in surplus and that as its running costs were being met largely out of public funds, it should stop collecting money from the Jewish community. Desmond dismissed such argument as foolish. There were children in need everywhere, he said, and urged that some of the surplus be used to establish a children's home in Jerusalem.

The idea for such a home came from the fertile brain of Alexander Russell, a pioneer in the diagnosis and treatment of handicapped children and Professor of Paediatrics at the Hadassah Hospital Medical School in Jerusalem. He envisaged a centre which would contain preventive, diagnostic, curative and rehabilitation facilities under one roof, as well as accommodation for parents who wished to be with their children while they were undergoing treatment. He took his scheme to the Mayor of Jerusalem, Teddy Kollek, who was charmed with it and promised to find an appropriate site in the centre of the City. However, there were no funds available to set the scheme in motion, so Kollek introduced Russell to Desmond.

Desmond was also taken with the idea in principle, but wanted further and better particulars. He questioned Russell: How much would it cost to build? What would be the running costs? What sort of building materials would be used? How would it work? How would the staff be recruited and trained? What would be the terms of employment and the salary scales? He even questioned Russell about the parking arrangements.

He felt that the paper plans did not tell him enough and commissioned a scale model at the cost of about £600. When Norwood refused to bear the cost, he paid for it out of his own pocket. He also visited the existing facilities and spoke to the staff, parents and children.

Russell was overwhelmed by his alacrity, his grasp of highly technical details and his personal sense of involvement. He has a particularly vivid memory of Desmond: tall, immaculate and grey-haired, getting down stiffly on his knees to play with the children.

Desmond discussed the matter with his executive and Norwood agreed to contribute £400,000 towards the cost, on the understanding that the rest would be found from local sources. But then came the first of a succession of hitches.

As soon as the proposals became known, letters began pouring into the *Jewish Chronicle* insisting that as Norwood was a local endowment, any surplus funds should be earmarked for local causes. Desmond was at first inclined to ignore such arguments, but lawyers were eventually consulted who pointed out that under the deed of trust Norwood money could be used only for the welfare of children in England and Wales. What added to the problem was Desmond's insistence, which he put in writing, that Arab children should also benefit from the scheme, whereas Norwood was a purely Jewish charity.

It was, in some ways, a distressing period for Desmond. He hated controversy and was used to having his way, but, having made a commitment to Kollek, he and his colleagues felt bound to honour it. They therefore launched a separate fund known as the Norwood Foundation, of which Desmond became President. Over a period of five years it raised £400,000 – the sum Desmond had initially pledged – for Russell's scheme. Russell assured him that neither he nor his colleagues had ever made any differentiation between Jew and Arab and never would, though Desmond insisted on having this in writing.

Kollek found a magnificent site on a hill overlooking the Knesset and building work began. However, costs spiralled and funds dried up before the building was completed, and it now stands an empty shell. Instead, an old building was found near the old Shaarei Tzedek hospital in the Jaffa Road and adapted for immediate use.

Professor Russell, a dapper, soft-spoken figure, with a billowing white moustache, still dreams that his plan will one day come to fruition, not only for the sake of the handicapped children but out of deference to Desmond's memory.

Desmond had also arranged for £5,000 a year to be paid to Jewish war orphans in Israel by Norwood, and in this instance too the money was paid out of the separate fund.

The new Norwood did not excite Desmond's affection quite as much as the old. The orphanage building, with its lead-latticed windows and pinnacled roof which had provided the charity with a corporate image, was no more, and gone with it were all the attendant echoes of the past. The children were scattered and no longer available for inspection, freshly scrubbed, in neat array on open day. The annual garden fête was likewise a thing of the past and the grandees who used to be associated with the charity were fewer in number and less frequently seen. Where ladies bountiful from good families were directly involved in the welfare of the children, the work was taken over by professionals. The socialites had given way to social workers.

Norwood was more streamlined and efficient, and the children themselves were certainly happier under the new set-up than the old one. In any case Norwood had grown too large to be manned by volunteers, no matter how well-meaning and dedicated. Although Desmond had to accept it, he was never entirely happy with it.

Here too Desmond the accountant was sometimes in conflict with Desmond the romantic, even though Desmond the accountant was largely responsible for many of the changes. He was Edwardian in appearance, in manner and at heart, and became more so after he was raised to the peerage; he had never reconciled himself to the fact that he had outlived the age of paternalism. Work for Norwood seemed like work and less like a moral imperative.

However, he never neglected his duties. Sidney Frosh, a Vice-President of Norwood who worked with him over many years, described him as indefatigable: 'If you had a problem to discuss, he was always available no matter how busy he was, at any time of the day or night. Don't know how he found the time. And very painstaking, especially when it came to finding the right man for the right job. He had sound judgement, which is why we kept calling him, and a firm hand.' Another associate, Ralph de Groot, spoke of him in similar terms: 'The thing about Desmond was that he could sum up a situation at a glance and get to the heart of a problem in a minute so that we kept calling on him at all times.'

Desmond finally stood down in 1983. Looking back on his years with the organisation, he wrote:

> It is hard now to remember a time when I was not associated with Norwood in one capacity or another. It has been part of my life and it is with the deepest regret that I announce my retirement as your President.
>
> There have been difficult years, exciting years, but there has never been a time when I failed to share with my Norwood colleagues the pleasure of helping Jewish

Holidaying in Bad Ragaz, Desmond was touched by the sight
of this young orphan girl

children who needed care. Perhaps what has given me the greatest satisfaction has been to see Norwood grow in experience and in its skills. There is no doubt in my mind that Norwood Child Care today is a welfare agency of which the whole Jewish community can be proud. Certainly I take pride in its professionalism, the quality of its care and the contribution it makes to Jewish family life.

It has been my privilege to be of service to Norwood and to share this responsibility with so many able and generous people. . . .

Finally; I would like to pay tribute to everyone who has supported our work financially. We could not sustain our care for Jewish children without their generosity.

To which one must add that in money terms, at least, he was not particularly generous himself, at least not to Norwood.

He suffered some embarrassment in 1975 when the *Jewish Chronicle* carried a report that he had donated £5,000 to a Jewish children's home in Manchester, and someone took the trouble to point out that the money wasn't his but Norwood's.

Traditionally the honorary officers of the principal Jewish charities gave of both their time and their money. Desmond gave mainly of his time, if only because – certainly compared to the Rothschilds and the Bearsteads – he was not a wealthy man, and though he was fairly well off by any other standards, he never felt financially secure. Betty Arkell, who all but worshipped him and believed that he embraced every human virtue, admitted, on reflection, that 'he was not a generous man, not where money was concerned,' which, coming from her, was tantamount to the suggestion that he was mean.

When he died, he failed to make special provisions for

Norwood. In a will he drew up in 1987 he did not leave Norwood a penny. By 1992 he had relented sufficiently to make some provision for it, but treated it no differently from Jewish Care, UNICEF, Imperial Cancer Research and half-a-dozen other charities. The sums involved, moreover, were not specified and would become available only as the residue of a trust fund on the death of his stepson. In other words, if he did not forget Norwood, he did not go out of his way to remember it.

Bronia believes that he fell out with Norwood at some point. However, Frosh has no recollection of a contretemps: 'Desmond, even under pressure, was courteous, considerate and genial, a pleasure to work with, and he certainly gave me the impression that he was devoted to Norwood.' The answer may have lain in the vexed relationship between Desmond and Sidney Bloch, the Chairman of Norwood who effectively functioned as Chief Executive. They were as different in personality as they were in their build. Desmond was very tall while Bloch was very short; encountered together they looked almost comical.

Bloch was a self-made man but, unlike Desmond, he had made enough money to retire at fifty and devote the rest of his life to social welfare. He became Chairman of Norwood in 1980 and, once installed, he more or less made it his full-time job. Desmond liked time to think whereas Bloch was in a hurry, as if he had not much time left. He died a few years later at the age of sixty-six. Desmond, with his extensive experience of government boards, was a stickler for precedent; Bloch made up his own rules as he went along. Desmond as President expected to be consulted on policy; Bloch was not much given to consulting anyone (to which one must add that Desmond, as head of HHI, was often out of the country and was not always available for consultation). Desmond liked to stand on his dignity; Bloch was no respecter of persons or personages (though he made an exception for the Queen).

When Desmond finally retired, many tributes were paid to his work and he was presented with a large silver salver by his colleagues. However, as the elder statesman of the organisation with a lifetime of service behind him, he assumed he would be informed about any major changes that were contemplated. He wasn't, and came to feel that enough was enough. He had retired from HHI at about the same time and believed that he had been ill-treated by them. In his darker moments he began to think that they were all jealous of him, his achievements, his foresight and his vision.

12

In Retirement

After Desmond retired from business in 1984 (though he was still Hon. Life President of HHI, and enjoyed short trips to France and Zürich, and still had personal clients), the House of Lords became his second home. He was there every day when the House was sitting and felt slightly lost when it was in recess. There were other figures like him around: tall, white-haired, slow-moving and dignified. He was seventy-one and had by almost imperceptible degrees become one of the Boys of the Old Brigade.

There was an attendance allowance of £30 a day and a secretarial allowance of a further £30, which to some peers was an important source of income. But Desmond came every day because he loved the place – the unhurried atmosphere, the tapestried walls, the book-lined corridors, the red upholstery, the gilded trappings, the vaulted ceilings, the lofty halls and the famous names, some because of their family history, others because of their achievements. It was a tranquil and constant scene in a troubled and inconstant world. It gave him peace of mind and sustained his morale. It also served as a reassuring reminder that he had got somewhere in life.

There were over a thousand peers in the country. Some three hundred might be found in the House in the course of a normal working day. Some had inherited their titles, some held government office, but most, like Desmond, had occupied senior positions in government, industry, commerce, academic life, the civil service and the professions. Now, in their twilight years, some of them felt like forgotten men, but as a group they were still a power in the land.

The House offered something of a finishing education. The debates were less gladiatorial than in 'the other place', and when a member rose to speak it was generally because he had something to say and not because he was anxious to score political points. The range of experience and expertise offered by the House, and especially by the life peers, was perhaps unique. There was something to be learned from almost every speech, and Desmond was a keen student.

Desmond had belonged to the Playboy Club because it was one of his clients. He also belonged to the RAC because he liked to use its swimming-pool, but he was not really a clubman. However, he found the House of Lords an excellent place to entertain. It had unrivalled facilities, was conveniently situated and it particularly impressed overseas guests. He received a steady flow of visitors from America, Canada, India, Japan, China, Israel, Egypt and the more outlying parts of the HHI empire, and he took particular pleasure not only in entertaining them to meals but in giving them a guided tour round the House. He also used the House of Lords as his office, even though he had a well-equipped study at home, and conducted his business correspondence on House of Lords writing-paper.

It was also his show-place. There was an annual exhibition of paintings in the Lords by members of both Houses of Parliament, and Desmond, until his last year, was one of the leading participants. The exhibition attracted a large crowd – apart from anything else, Bronia could always be counted upon to mobilise their many friends – and considerable attention, and he was always excited by the number of pictures he sold, not because he needed the money – which in any case went to charity – but because a purchase was the sincerest form of approval.

There are no reserved places in the Lords except for members of the front bench and ex-Prime Ministers, and Desmond's own favourite perch, to which he acquired an almost proprietorial attitude, was in the second row beyond the gangway behind Lord Callaghan, not because he liked to be near the famous – though he did – but because by 1984 he was walking with the aid of a stick and ascending even one step called for some effort. In any case he was a good friend of Lord Callaghan and their propinquity allowed an opportunity for a chat. Lord Shinwell had offered his seat to Desmond.

There were about a hundred Labour peers and during term Party Whips called about one meeting a week to consider policy and tactics. During his first years in the House, as we have seen, Desmond occasionally questioned the Party line and might even oppose it in debate, but in his later years he caused no trouble, not because his views had changed but because it was the age of Margaret Thatcher. Labour was in opposition and seemed doomed to remain so for some years to come, and he might have felt that it was not a time to rock the boat. In any case, he had already made his views clear and he was disinclined to repeat himself.

Lord Graham of Edmonton, the Labour Chief Whip, a

kind, amiable figure, recalls him as 'a good, Party man, dependable, reliable, loyal. Very informed', he added, 'and full of ideas. Callaghan often picked his brains. We all did. Not only knew a lot, but could take you straight to the heart of a problem. Good man to have around. Great asset to the Party. We loved him.'

Desmond was a member of the All-Party Select Committee on European Affairs, which had about fifteen members. It met about once a fortnight while the House was in session, and he made his presence felt as an authority on currency and public finance. Although he attended debates regularly, he never actually spoke. There is some mystery in the fact that during his first years in the House, when he was still senior partner in HHH, with many demands on his time, he spoke frequently, whereas after he retired he never spoke at all.

He was in declining health, but he still addressed HHI gatherings and charity dinners. He was, however, the star turn at such occasions, whereas in the Lords he was among men and women who were nearly all stars in their different fields. He was assured attention in the first, but had to jostle for it in the second. He was among fans in the former, among his peers in the latter. In HHI he could give the same speech in several different cities; he could not give the same speech twice in the Lords, though there were occasions – as on race relations, for example – when he came close to doing so.When he was a new man in the House he had felt under some compulsion to shine, if only to show that he was worthy of the honour he had received. As an old one, he could relax.

In his first years in the House, he had never missed an opportunity to remind listeners of the social and economic problems which would arise if the country did not face up to the challenge of automation. He hated change and, when he contemplated the brave new world ahead with machines taking over from men even in professional occupations, he would say with a sigh: 'Thank goodness I won't be around when it all happens,' though in fact he lived long enough to see some of his fears confirmed. Many of his warnings, even if they seemed wild at the time, had been justified by events, but he was not the sort of man to draw comfort from telling people 'I told you so', even if he drew reassurance from being proved right.

In earlier years, moreover, he had been on close terms with every Party leader from Attlee to Callaghan; and even if he was not a front bencher, he felt himself to be part of the ruling elite, which somehow added to his confidence. His very standing in the Party had placed him under some obligation to speak. However, he meant little to Michael Foot and Neil Kinnock, the new generation of Labour leaders, and they meant little to him. Speeches were an ordeal to him, but when the House debated an issue on which he felt particularly strongly, such as the War Crimes Bill in June 1990, he naturally took part. When he became unwell, getting to the House was a great pleasure, both relaxing and stimulating.

And finally, as we have noted, he might have felt disappointed by his omission from Wilson's resignation honours list. To be sure he already had a peerage, but his contribution to public life before 1967 did not compare with his contribution since, and he had been led to expect something more. Lord Shackleton had said to Desmond that he deserved an honour for all the work he had done in Chevening and on other committees.

Desmond was a man of habit, so regular that Bronia could time her watch by his movements. After rising, he listened to the news, bathed, shaved and dressed, slowly and deliberately He was, even in old age, fastidious about his appearance. He would join Bronia for breakfast at about

Rue Eugène Colas,
Deauville, Normandie

Deauville sketched in 1986

8.45. The fare was usually fresh orange-juice, toast, and a pot of coffee, which he would have with *The Times* or *Financial Times*. Bronia read the *Telegraph*, and they might exchange a few words about the headlines, which generally filled them with misgivings. The whole process was unhurried and it was nearly 10 o'clock before he finished.

The morning mail brought few excitements, usually charity appeals. Being a peer has its penalties. For all his forwarning about the impact of computers, he never used one himself. He never even had a typewriter or fax machine in his flat.

He still had business interests, but though he kept a careful eye on them, they were the sort which largely looked after themselves. He had no doubt that he would predecease Bronia and had set up two companies, Hillguard Limited and Woodmond Securities Limited, mainly for her benefit, to satisfy himself that whatever other difficulties she might have to face, her financial future would be secure.

Woodmond is a property company and derives its name from an association between Woodrow Wyatt and Desmond. Lord Wyatt owned a property which he was anxious to develop and turned to Desmond, a neighbour and friend, for advice. Desmond in turn brought in Ralph de Groot, a chartered surveyor, with whom he had worked over many years in the Norwood Foundation. They developed the Wyatt property and acquired others, and the undertaking flourished. Lord Wyatt later sold his share in the company and Desmond became the controlling shareholder, passing on his holding to Bronia.

Bronia lives comfortably on the income. 'No husband could have been more far-sighted or more caring. I was never out of his thoughts. I only wish he had taken more trouble to look after himself.'

He was a hoarder of personal memorabilia, letters from

this tailor, or that art dealer, letters of invitation, letters of thanks, letters of apology, birthday cards, Christmas cards, get-well cards, dinner menus, bills of lading, health records, visa applications, airline counterfoils, invitations to weddings, dinners, receptions, menus, even old school reports, all of them neatly indexed and filed. He added to the collection till the end of his days, still with the same careful sense of order.

He never collected a commonplace book, but scattered among his papers are poems, aphorisms, epigrams, bon-mots and stray pieces of folk wisdom which he used to embellish his speeches, including the following which he sometimes used as a grace before meals and which he would recite with a working-class accent:

> Give us, Lord, a bit o'sun,
> A bit o'work and a bit o'fun;
> Give us in all the struggle and sputter
> Our daily bread and a bit o'butter
> Give us our health, our keep to make,
> An a bit to spare for others' sake;
> Give us too a bit o'song
> and a tale and a book to help us along.
> Give us, Lord, a chance to be
> Our goodly best, brace wise and free.
> Our goodly best for ourselves and others,
> Till all men learn to live as brothers.

He was also a philatelist with a large and fairly valuable collection of first-day covers from all over the world, which filled several dozen albums. He would pore over them with quiet pleasure, for they not only evoked happy memories of the many places which he and Bronia had visited together during their travels but the boyhood years when he first began his collection.

At 12.30 he had a snack lunch with Bronia and would leave for the House an hour later. He never missed Question Time if he could help it, and – barring a major debate – would leave for home at 6 p.m. At 6.30 Bronia would be out on the front balcony looking out for his red Rolls. If he wasn't back by 6.45, she became anxious. If he wasn't back by 7, she was ready to call the police.

They now rarely entertained at home on weekdays, although Bronia sometimes invited a couple of friends for dinner to amuse Desmond. Usually, they would dine quietly together and afterwards would have a game of Scrabble in the study. They rarely watched television. On balmy summer evenings they had coffee on the balcony while the laughter of people at play came wafting up from the park below. And then, as dusk fell, they saw the blur of red lights of cars moving in one direction, and of white lights in the other.

Desmond liked to be in bed by eleven with a book, usually a political biography. His study is still lined with books on or by every leading politician of his day, British and American, and even minor ones where they happened to be members or ex-members of the Labour Party. He also had a considerable collection of Jewish books – histories, biographies and sacred texts – which he had accumulated in his younger years and which bore the marks of earnest study. He had a good memory and would sometimes surprise people with the extent of his Jewish knowledge.

He began attending synagogue on High Holy Days and occasional Saturdays, something he hadn't done since he was a schoolboy, though he now preferred the St John's Wood Synagogue to Hampstead. He would follow the service closely, and would sometimes pull the Rabbi – Dr Nisson Shulman – aside after the service to discuss some obscure point in the liturgy or Scripture. He also acquired the habit of saying a prayer before settling down to sleep. It didn't mean that he had become a born-again Jew, if only because he had never lapsed, but, like many old men, he found increasing comfort in tradition and religious observance. As for Bronia, she turned to God *in extremis*. Although from a strictly Orthodox home, Bronia was much less observant. She rarely set foot in synagogue or opened a prayer book, but when faced with a crisis, no rabbi in England was Orthodox enough for her and she would rush to some Hassidic sage in Jerusalem.

In his younger years Desmond used to enjoy a game of golf, usually on a Sunday morning, but could no longer summon the necessary energy. Now he liked to spend Sunday with his sister Joan and her husband Eric. They had a spacious home with a large garden in Esher and would be joined by their children and a large contingent of grandchildren.

They were lively, even boisterous, occasions, but Desmond enjoyed the company of young people and was particularly fond of Joan's daughters. One of them, Anne Sebba, later recalled: 'As an uncle he was kind, generous and unflaggingly interested in the activities of the younger generation.'

Bronia's son, Frank, who had been a source of anxiety in his younger years, had finally found stability and contentment. Although Frank and Desmond had always had a good relationship, Desmond had been disappointed that Frank had left university before getting a degree and had not wanted to take up the place Desmond had offered him in his accountancy practice. Instead, Frank had gone to Avignon in France, where, through his love of sport, especially tennis and skiing, he had set up a sports club, which was flourishing. He had also been given a small catering company in London by his father, which had proved successful. In 1976, however, he had had a serious car accident, which had left him disabled. Fortunately he had been able to pull himself together sufficiently to continue these businesses. Later, he also took a diploma in jewellery design and the study of diamonds.

Desmond had made generous provisions for him in his will, but none for his children. Frank had married out of the faith, not once but twice. Desmond felt even more strongly about these things than Bronia, who stemmed from strict rabbinic stock. Frank, however, was too much a man of principle to expect his wives or children to conform to a faith he had abandoned.

Desmond and Bronia went to the theatre a lot and were particularly fond of concerts, the opera and the ballet. They would also eat out from time to time. They managed the occasional excursion to their beloved Paris, eating in good restaurants, haggling over paintings in galleries, searching for bargains in dusty antique shops, strolling in the Bois de Boulogne, and recalling their yesterdays.

The major events in their year were their anniversaries, Desmond's birthday in May, Bronia's birthday in November and, most important of all, their wedding anniversary in July, which Desmond always marked with letters of appreciation. The terms were usually the same – 'My Dearest Darling. To a Great and Wonderful Wife, with grateful thanks for the happiness you have brought me . . . for all you have done for me . . . for the love and warmth you have brought into my life.' Bronia couldn't read them often enough, especially as Desmond was rather more effusive in writing than in speech, but possibly her most cherished moments were the unexpected ones, when she looked up from a book to find him watching her with affectionate contemplation.

Desmond and Bronia did everything together, not only because they happened to be particularly devoted to each other, but also because there was virtually no one else whose company they particularly wanted. As a pair they were more or less self-sufficient.

13

The Final Years

Desmond was ailing, but he was still very proud and in command of his body and his looks. Bronia had quite a few problems of her own to contend with, as one can see from a light-hearted card which Desmond sent her: 'To my Darling Angel, and Brave Goddess – in spite of trouble with rheumatism. But what a great girl. With all these problems and ME! Quite marvellous. From your adoring darling with love and affection.'

But if he could make light of her infirmities, she could not make light of his. He had been plagued by respiratory ailments all his life, which gradually had a debilitating effect on his heart. He tired easily and had difficulty in walking. What made it worse was his addiction to tobacco in all its forms, cigars, cigarettes and a pipe. Bronia hated to nag – and more particularly Desmond hated to be nagged – so she suffered in silence. His doctors finally made him stop, but by then it was too late. To his frequent bouts of bronchitis there was added a failing heart.

He had his first heart attack in the 1970s. Then, some months afterwards, doctors found an infection in one of his hips. When he went in for surgery for a hip replacement, the anaesthetist warned Bronia that his weak heart and clogged arteries would make the operation extremely hazardous. 'It's a twenty-five per cent chance – if that,' he said. Bronia immediately contacted Hassidic rabbis in Jerusalem and asked them for prayers and advice. They assured her that the operation would succeed.

In April 1988 he received a letter from Merlyn Rees MP, a former Home Secretary and old friend, inviting him to join an All Party War Crimes Group. He replied a few weeks later:

> In earlier times I was extremely active in the Refugee Organisations and had very much to do with rescuing political and religious people who suffered under the Nazi regime. Unfortunately, I am going through a very painful patch physically. Acute arthritis of both hips have reached a point where movement has become severely restricted and painful. I am to undergo hip replacement surgery shortly. I can hardly lend any active support to the All Party War Crimes Group for the time being; but as a token of my wishing to help, I enclose a contribution.

He still continued to attend the Lords, however, hobbling around with difficulty, and one afternoon Lord Shackleton found him slumped on a bench in one of the corridors. He called Baroness Birk, a friend of the family, who took one look at him and called a nurse. The nurse called an ambulance and he was rushed to Westminster Hospital, where they diagnosed a heart attack. Lady Birk, who had accompanied him to hospital, had to break the news to Bronia.

Bronia rushed to the hospital and remained there for the

week he was in intensive care, feeding him, nursing him, keeping callers at bay and reading the papers to him. By the time he recovered, she herself was on the point of collapse.

It was the second of three such attacks, the last of which was to prove fatal. In each case Bronia took a room next to his, as she did every time he required surgery, and the medical staff found themselves coping not only with a very sick patient but with very a overwrought spouse.

She felt that Desmond needed her, and her alone, and was reassured when she was there – by his side. In any case she couldn't trust anyone else to see to him with sufficient care, an attitude which did not endear her to either the doctors or the nurses. Indeed, whenever Desmond fell ill, Bronia was not the only one to greet the news with alarm. She was not impervious to the impression she made, but she didn't care. Her love for her husband transcended all other considerations. Desmond's stay in hospital was covered by health insurance; Bronia's was not, and it cost a fortune.

On 11 November 1992, on her seventy-seventh birthday, he gave her a birthday card with the inscription:

My Darling,
   May God thank you always, and grant you many more years of activity and interest, freed from much of the pains you have sadly suffered through so many causes. May we both be spared for many years to comfort each other and help each other in difficult times. I thank you for all your wonderful help, kindness and love during a year when I have experienced physical upsets and pain.

Bronia was patient, understanding and forgiving, but Desmond remained distressed. He was overwhelmed by a sense of futility. 'What's it all about?' he would ask himself. 'What am I doing here?' He was often in tears, yet he could also be fun and jolly.

Then in April 1993 his sister Joan died. She was only seventy. He had grown distant from his brother, but remained close to Joan, who, even in her late sixties, retained her startling good looks, her sparkling personality and sunny nature. They had met at least once a week and her company evoked happy memories of their adolescent years in The Ridgeway, Golders Green, with the french windows in the drawing-room opening out on to clipped lawns, like the setting for a Noël Coward comedy, the boisterous presence of his mother, the cheerful chatter of young friends, tennis parties, theatre outings, picnics in the country, motor rallies, dinners, dances, and the Coronation ball with Joan, then only seventeen, as the reigning queen. She was distressed by the tensions which had developed between Desmond and his brother, could never quite understand them and made repeated efforts to reconcile them, but with limited success.

'Joan', as Bronia recalls, 'was everybody's darling', but she sometimes resented her because when she was around, Desmond rarely had time for anyone else, and she herself sometimes felt like an outsider. When Joan died, Desmond lost the will to live.

Bronia thought that he might enjoy a visit to Bad Ragaz or Davos, his favourite Swiss resorts, but that would have meant wheelchairs and transfers. Instead, they took the ferry to France and stayed at the Westminster Hotel in Le Touquet. It was their last holiday together and not a happy one. The skies were grey, the air was moist and cold, the winds were shrill, seagulls shrieked and the seas pounded angrily on the empty shore.

Bronia had packed an easel and canvas in the hope that she might induce Desmond to paint, but they could not venture out of doors, and he remained propped up in a large chair gazing glumly at the bleak scene. He left his gourmet meals untouched, his wine undrunk. When they returned to London, he succumbed to a severe bronchial complaint.

Though Desmond had been retired for a few years, his name still carried weight within the trade union movement and in October 1993 he was invited by the National Union of Journalists to intervene in a dispute between the editorial staff and management of the *Jewish Chronicle*. As always he liked to be helpful and replied to say that he would do what he could. It was his last letter, for by then he was too ill to do anything at all. A few weeks later he had another attack. He had his third heart attack on 6 December 1993 and this time, although Bronia tried to give him the kiss of life, he could not be resuscitated. 'He died holding me,' says Bronia, 'very peacefully.'

He was rushed to University College Hospital and was found to be dead on arrival. Bronia refused to allow his body to be moved to the mortuary. Rabbi Shulman, who was with her, assured her that he would sit by the body through the night. She wouldn't listen. The nurses summoned a superintendent, who threatened to throw her out of the hospital, but she had been thrown out before and she didn't care. She wanted him home.

He was propped up and strapped into a wheelchair, a private ambulance was summoned and she took him back to Imperial Court. The porters were alerted and they wheeled him across the lobby to the lift, and then up seven floors to her flat, and put him to bed – not on the bed but in it – and Bronia tucked him in as if to assure him a good night's sleep. Later a crowd of friends came to pay their respects.

Rabbi Shulman arrived with his wife Rivka to keep Bronia company through the night, but she wanted to be alone with Desmond. She had not quite reconciled herself to the thought that he was dead and spent the night lying on the bed beside him. Rabbi Shulman returned the next morning with the Chevra Kadisha, the Jewish burial society, to perform the last rites.

The funeral, the letters of condolence, the service, kept Bronia frantically busy, but when they were all over she was desolated.

The tributes to him both private and public were many and warmhearted. There were lengthy obituaries in every major paper. Letters poured in from all over the world from friends and colleagues who had known him at various points in his career, and from mere strangers who had been helped by him and had cause to revere his memory.

Desmond had left no requests on the matter and the fact that his memorial service was held in the House of Lords rather than in St John's Wood Synagogue was Bronia's doing. It was not that she necessarily preferred to think of him as a Lord rather than as a Jew, but that Desmond had always been a Jew, while Desmond the Lord was a product of their partnership. Moreover, the House was the setting of his apotheosis and the symbol of his triumphs.

Rabbi Shulman, who had only got to know him late in life, possibly spoke for them all at the memorial meeting: 'He saw all people as equal. So he worked all his life for the betterment of the working man, for his security, for his welfare, for the party that would benefit him or her. . . . He saw the uniqueness of each human being. In this, I suggest he was inspired by his artist's eye. He perceived that charity, especially for children, can help develop this uniqueness, and bring out gifts that otherwise might be hidden and dormant. . . . He saw the infinite importance of each human being; each a potential world. And when movements arose that destroyed human life, he sought to save lives and succeeded many times.'

It was a perceptive summary of a remarkable career.

Desmond, as he made clear in more than one House of Lords' debate, was a proud and loyal Jew, if not a particularly devout one. He never conformed to the minutiae of Jewish observance and, for example, disregarded the dietary laws, but he did conform to the major precepts of the faith and especially the obligation to care for the poor, the sick and the maimed. Throughout his life he had helped the needy, the old and the young.

Though he lived in a libidinous age, he was – certainly where Bronia was concerned – a faithful and devoted husband, and though he may have brought her worries in abundance on other matters, she had none as far as his fidelity was concerned. Apart from anything else, she was perfectly convinced, probably with justification, that she met all his needs. He often warned that increased leisure could lead to increased licentiousness, even depravity, but, though his warnings were amply confirmed by events, he was never censorious. He combined a relish for low gossip with distaste for sleaze, and was at once amused by the ways of the world and disturbed by them. His own conduct, however, was shaped not so much by moral fastidiousness as by self-respect.

He was one of the pillars, and indeed one of the ornaments, of the Jewish community, but he needed a wider outlet for his energies and found it in the Labour movement and the Labour Party. He was sometimes at odds with Labour policy, but shared its humanitarian ideals and welcomed the scope it offered to display his very considerable abilities as a manager and financial administrator.

He was a little disappointed with the conservatism of the Labour Party and the trade unions and failed to imbue them with a sense of urgency about the impact of automation, or more than temper their traditional hostility to capitalism, but then he was ahead of his time. Had he lived a little longer, he would have been cheered by the spectacle of a Labour leader actually wooing the City.

By the time most men are sixty-two they are content to contemplate the prospect of retirement, but Desmond wasn't. He was a great success as President of HHI and showed himself to be a super-salesman and popular ambassador at large, but even with the scope which the job offered for international travel, lavish entertainment and lavish display – all of which he loved – it was hardly compensation for all the opportunities he thought he had missed. As a result, he sometimes felt embittered towards the end of his life.

And yet, among his disappointments and setbacks, he had many blessings: a wonderfully happy marriage, a vast circle of friends, an even larger circle of admirers, an enviable lifestyle, a proud record of public service and a lifetime of achievement.

A meticulous diarist, Desmond built up over the years a fascinating record of his public life and private observations. His diaries and photographs are now in the Labour Party archives in Manchester. He also loved to use a cine camera and the film he shot on his regular visits to Israel from the 1930s onwards – an invaluable record of the birth and infancy of a nation – now forms a significant contribution to the Speilberg archives in the Museum of Jerusalem.

Desmond's achievements speak for themselves. For the son of an unqualified dentist who left school at sixteen, he could be forgiven for thinking that he had done well for himself but, not content with that, he could draw comfort from the thought that he had done well for others. In particular – which brings us to his main quality – he could claim to have been a visionary.

Desmond often used to jot down appropriate sayings on a notepad, one of which could sum up his attitude to life:

Life's Race is well run,
Life's Work is well done,
Life's Crown is well won,
The rest in peace
with God everlasting.

Desmond was fairly familiar with Scripture and as we know he chose his motto, 'Come now let and us reason together', from Isaiah, and he lived up to it. But there is also a passage from the Talmud which, though too long to fit neatly under a heraldic crest, might have summed up his philosophy of life: 'The day is short, the task demanding, the labourers are sluggish, the reward is great, and the master is impatient. It is not thy duty to complete the task, but neither art thou free to desist from it.'

Epilogue

BY BRONIA HIRSHFIELD

Life with my dear husband was always interesting, but on the few occasions when I could see boredom on the horizon, I felt it incumbent on me to add some excitement.

Occasionally solutions to Desmond's professional problems were found not by cool, rational analysis, but by my 'woman's intuition' linked with a touch of laughter. At the end of the day he loved to relax with small talk, gossip, *Dad's Army* on television and a good meal. Even a game of Scrabble helped.

During HHI conferences, it was often my duty – as well as my pleasure – to mix with many partners' wives from all over the world. As wife of the senior international partner and as these conferences often affected policy (indeed, in some third world countries even government economic policy), I took the ups and downs of my function very seriously, hoping that the wives had as good a time as their husbands.

We travelled to many conventions and Desmond also took me along to many individual meetings. I acted as linguist, hostess, speech reader and observer – all roles undertaken with love and dedication.

Some of these episodes can now be seen as humorous, but at the time they were far from such. What does one do when a plane lands in Malaysia in the middle of nowhere at midnight, and when the reception committee speaks not a word of any European language and offers us very questionable transport? For a moment I thought that we were about to be kidnapped because at that particular time Malaysia and Britain were not on friendly terms. On another occasion, at an economic seminar, we landed late in Jakarta and were forcibly separated on arrival, with Desmond and his suitcase going in one direction and me in another. It transpired that the conference was already assembled and awaiting Desmond's speech, and no time was to be lost. Meanwhile I was taken to the hotel and was again convinced that Desmond had been abducted. Experiences like these have to be borne; later one can see the funny side of things.

It has always struck me that a wife at home, in surroundings that are familiar, is in charge of day-to-day events and is mistress of her destiny. However, a wife in unfamiliar and often dangerous surroundings must ensure that the purpose of the visit is achieved. I believe that for the most part Desmond and I succeeded.

During our travels I realised that, as well as my deep love for him, I had great admiration and respect for his work, his clear brain and way of thinking, and his successful handling of difficult situations.

Index

Index

2994

my boss